LONDON RECORD SOCIETY PUBLICATIONS

VOLUME XLIV

Clive Burgess

29. x. 09

THE PINNERS' AND WIRESELLERS' BOOK 1462–1511

EDITED BY

BARBARA MEGSON

LONDON RECORD SOCIETY
2009

ISBN: 978-0-900952-44-9

Typeset, printed and bound by
Winstonmead Print, Loughborough, Leics

CONTENTS

ABBREVIATIONS

BL	British Library
CCR	*Calendar of Close Rolls*
CPMR	*Calendar of Plea and Memoranda Rolls of the City of London,* ed. A.H.Thomas, vols. 1–4; ed. Philip E. Jones, vols. 5–6 (Cambridge, 1924–1961)
CPR	*Calendar of Patent Rolls*
Ekwall	*Two Early London Subsidy Roll*s, ed. E. Ekwall (Lund, 1951)
EcHR	*Economic History Review*
GL	Guildhall Library
HW	*Calendar of Wills Proved and Enrolled in the Court of Husting, London 1258–1688,* ed. R.R.Sharpe, 2 vols. (London, 1899–90)
L.Arch.	GL; Register of Wills proved in the Archdeaconry Court of London
LB [A-L]	*Calendar of Letter Books of the City of London, A-L*, ed. R.R.Sharpe, 11 vols. (London, 1899–1912)
L.Com.	GL; Register of Wills proved in the Commissary Court of London
LJ	*London Journal*
Memorials	*Memorials of London and London Life*, ed. H.T.Riley (London, 1868)
Reps	Repertories: Manuscript series in City of London Record Office
RP	*Rotuli Parliamentorum 1278–1503*, 6 vols. (London, 1832)
SR	*The Statutes of the Realm*, 10 vols. (London, 1810–28)
TNA	The National Archives
Unwin	G. Unwin, *The Guilds and Companies of London* (London, 1908)

ACKNOWLEDGEMENTS

In the course of compiling this version of the Pinners' and Wiresellers' Book, I have become indebted to a number of people. In particular to Drs Stephen O'Connor and Vanessa Harding, the editors of this series, for their advice and forebearance on many matters. I am also most grateful to Dr Matthew Davies for drawing my attention to the early lease of a property owned by the Merchant Taylors' Company, to Dr Hannes Kleineke for giving me two references to pinners, one in the Court of Common Pleas and the other in the Court of King's Bench, and to Dr Anne Sutton who invited me to draw on her notes on the Wardrobe Accounts. I should also record my gratitude to my good friend, Harold Barkley for many hours spent in proof reading with me: and to Dr Anne Cobby for timely assistance with the transcription and translation of the original pinners' articles in Norman French. Finally I must thank Professor Caroline Barron, not only for telling me of the existence of the Pinners' and Wiresellers' Book but also for reading the introduction to it and making many helpful comments thereon, and for her valuable assistance with the index.

Barbara Megson
January 2009

INTRODUCTION

The Pinners' Book (BL MS Egerton 1142) now rests in the British Library. An entry on the second sheet in the new binding records that it was purchased on 16 October 1846 from I. B. Nicholls, Esq. Its chief purpose was that of an audit book, recording the biennial accounts made by the outgoing wardens at the end of their two-year term of office. The first accounts cover the years 1462–1464 and the volume continued to be used for this purpose even after 1497, when the Pinners amalgamated with the Wiredrawers, to become the new company of the Wiresellers. The last entry is dated 1511.

The first accounts cover the years 1462–1464 and the book may well have been begun as a result of the 'Charter' of 1463, in which Edward IV responded to the petitions of many small 'luxury' crafts for protection from the competition of increasing imports of similar foreign goods.[1] With royal protection thus assured, the Pinners took steps to set their affairs in order and, if possible, to establish themselves as a craft of recognised standing.[2]

The Pinners' first action was to have an exemplification of the new 'Charter' made, as a safeguard, lest royal or civic authority later overlooked it and this, together with a copy of their original ordinances of 1356, were the first items to be entered in their new book (**1–2**). A calendar was also specially purchased, at a cost of 10d. and this was duly bound into the front of their new book (**4**).

The survival of such early craft accounts is rare. Apart from those held by some of the major merchant companies, only three sets of accounts for lesser crafts are known to have survived from the fifteenth century.[3] Of these, only the accounts of the Carpenters have been published, although detailed histories of the other two crafts, the Pewterers and the Cutlers,

1. This was not a new problem. In 1440 there had been complaints when two Venetian galleys called at Southampton that year importing a total of 83,000 pins, see H.S.Cobb, 'Cloth Exports from London and Southampton in the Later Fifteenth and Early Sixteenth Centuries: A Revision', *EcHR*, 2nd ser., vol. xxxi (1978), pp. 601–9.
2. 1463, 3 Edward IV c.4, *SR*, vol. 2, pp. 396–98.
3. Bower Marsh ed., *Records of the Worshipful Company of Carpenters*, vol. 2 (Oxford, 1914): Wardens' Account Book 1438–1516 (Oxford, 1914); Charles Welch, *History of the Worshipful Company of Pewterers of London*, 2 vols. (London, 1902); Thomas H. Girtin, *The Mark of the Sword: a Narrative History of the Cutlers' Company 1189–1975* (London, 1975).

have been written based on their records. To date, there has been no such study of the craft of Pinners, although George Unwin, as early as 1908, drew upon their book extensively in writing his seminal *The Guilds and Companies of London.*

Of the Pinners' craft very little other evidence remains: the original ordinances of 1356, in Anglo-Norman, were inscribed in the London Letter Book G, making it possible to compare them with the later version in the Pinners' Book.[4] There are a few references to individuals in the later Letter Books of the City of London, scraps of information occasionally appear in the records of the London mayor's court and there are twenty-eight pinners' wills, mainly proved in the London Commissary Court. The earliest surviving will is that of John atte Hill dated 1395 **(69)**. The paucity of evidence serves to highlight the value of this Pinners' book covering the years from 1462 to 1511.[5]

EARLY HISTORY OF THE PINNERS' CRAFT, 1278–1356

Though not formally recognised as a city craft until 1356, pinners must have been working in London for many generations before this date. Walter le Pinnere was recorded as living in the parish of St. Bartholomew, Smithfield, in 1278 and appears there again, as a mainpernour, in 1281. Will le Pynnere appeared in the ward of Bishopsgate in 1292, as a contibutor to the lay subsidy. In 1338 Richard le Pinnere was recorded as one of those from the ward of Castle Baynard chosen and sworn to safeguard the city from possible French invasion.[6]

The origins of the pin are lost in prehistory. Pins have been found, not only in Iron Age Britain, but also in the more ancient civilisations of Assyria, Egypt, Greece and Rome, used to secure the draped clothing worn, in various forms, by all these peoples. These early pins were made of bone, forged iron and copper but, some time after the end of the Roman Empire, the art of wire-drawing developed and from then on wire was the basic material for pin making. This enabled the pinners to produce pins with finer shanks and smaller heads than hitherto.[7]

The process, though relatively simple, was tripartite and involved a range of skills. First the brass wire shank had to be polished and sharpened on a

4. *LBG*, pp. 63–4.
5. For a list of surviving pinners' and wiresellers' wills see Appendix 1.
6. Ekwall, p. 189; *LBB*, pp. 11, 279; *LBF*, p. 21.
7. For further information on the history of pins see: Reginald Higgins, *Jewellery from Classical Lands* (London, 1969), pp. 11–30; Norman Pounds, *An Economic History of Medieval Europe* (London, 1994), pp. 400–402, 453; Arthur MacGregor, 'Antler, Bone and Horn' in John Blair and Nigel Ramsay eds., *English Medieval Industries: Craftsmen, Techniques, Products* (London, 1991), pp. 355–78 esp. p. 370; Geoffrey Egan and Frances Pritchard, *Dress Accessories 1150–1450*, 2nd edn (Woodbridge, 2002), pp. 297–304.

knuckle bone. Attaching the head was a more complex process. First a piece of wire was wound round the upper part of the shank and soldered on to form a collar. The pin head, finely bored to fit, was then put in place and soldered on.[8] Once perfected, these processes changed little and were precisely described in 'An Acte for the true making of Pynnes' of 1544. Standard pins were there defined as 'oonelie suche as shalbe double headed and have the heades soudered faste to the Shanke of the Pynne well smethed, the Shanke well shaven the pointe well and round fyled cauted and sharped...'[9]

Lists of customs duties paid at the ports testify to the fact that, from as early as 1228, iron ore had been imported from central Europe. The English metal-working industry was booming in the fourteenth century, partly through the demand for munitions in the war against France. The pinners, though one of its lowliest branches, also benefited from a growing demand for their product: not by cause of war but of fashion. The clothes of the period reflected the improving standards of living: in particular, the elaborate swathed head-dresses of fashionable court and London ladies, which were kept in place, over wire frames, by pins. The young Princess Joan, daughter of King Edward III, included 12,000 pins in her trousseau in 1348. The accounts of the King's Wardrobe recorded large orders of pins for both the royal family and courtiers at this time: and, as the Pinners' Book shows, nuns also used many quantities of pins to secure their enshrouding head-dresses (**8**). The fashion continued into the fifteenth century when a new type of metal, Osmund ore from Sweden, greatly improved the work of the wiredrawer and the pinners.[10]

By 1356, the craft was in a position to present its ordinances at Guildhall for acceptance as an accredited mystery of the City. Until then, the pinners had almost certainly formed a loose association with other allied trades. The early appearance of their ordinances may have been precipitated by a rift between them and the cardmakers, who produced bats stuck with nails or pins for carding wool.[11] Such conflicts between fellow craftsmen were common and usually led to the formation of one or more separate mysteries.[12]

Sometimes craftsmen fell out among themselves. An entry in the mayor's court roll of 1364 recorded that 'certain unnamed pinners were mainprised

8. Claude Blair and John Blair, 'Copper Alloys' in Blair and Ramsay eds., *English Medieval Industries*, pp. 81–106.
9. 1542–3, 34 & 35 Henry VIII c.6, *SR*, vol. 3, p. 904.
10. Jane Geddes, 'Iron' in Blair and Ramsay eds., *English Medieval Industries*, pp. 167–88, esp. pp. 169, 172–3, 182.
11. Heather Swanson, *Medieval Artisans* (Oxford, 1989), p. 72
12. For a typical conflict between the Bowyers and Fletchers in 1371, see: B. E. Megson, *Such Goodly Company: A Glimpse of the Life of the Bowyers of London 1300–1600* (London, 1993), pp. 24–25

to pay a fine of 40s. to the Chamber. William de Brakelee, pinner was mainprised to keep the peace with John Sharp, pinner...'[13]

THE ORDINANCES OF 1356: GOVERNANCE AND ADMINISTRATION

For one of the humbler crafts, the pinners registered their ordinances early, in 1356. The ordinances were designed to regulate the mystery which exercised its right to establish standards of workmanship and hours of work and to enforce them through the overall supervision by the craft of the product and its sale. Where more than one craft was involved in such supervision, disputes over the inspection of one skill by another were almost inevitable. The cardmakers would not welcome the surveillance of those who made pins, and vice versa.

When, in 1462, the pinners reorganised their affairs, they preceded the audit records with the two documents which justified their existence: a copy of the statute of 1463 conceding the points of their recent petition, known as the 'Charter', and a full copy of their fourteenth-century ordinances. This version of the ordinances may well have been copied from the entry in the city's Letter Book since there is little difference between the fifteenth-century English version and the original Anglo-Norman text.

There was a certain similarity in the ordinances of most crafts since they implicitly endorsed many long-established customs and rules already existing in the city. Each craft sought to protect itself from interlopers and to restrict the making of their products to their own members. Foreign (i.e. non citizen) pinners from outside the city of London could only exercise their skills after submitting their workmanship to the scrutiny of the craft wardens and, thereafter, on payment of a fine to join the brotherhood. In due course, if they could raise the money, they might rise from the position of a workman to that of a full brother and thence purchase for themselves the right to the freedom of the city, the status of master and the right to run a workshop and to train apprentices.

There were also prohibitions for the masters: against the poaching of fellow members' workmen and apprentices, for example, and the usual *caveat* that only a master might take on an apprentice. Poor workmanship and forestalling of goods would result in their destruction. It is of interest that women workers were acceptable members of the fraternity, even as workwomen but, as the ordinances expressly state, this privilege was only extended to the wives and daughters of members of the craft. As the city required, the craft accepted responsibility not only for the quality of workmanship of its members but also for their behaviour as citizens in general.

13. *CPMR 1323–1364*, p. 272.

On the other hand, the craft undertook to support its covenanted workmen in times of illness until they were able to work again.

All these duties were carried out under the supervision of wardens elected every two years. At the election the accounts of the previous wardens would be presented and audited. The record of these audits is the origin of this book. On this occasion the wardens would receive, under bond, a proportion of the money belonging to the craft, transferred to them by their predecessors to hold in trust during their period of office.

There is no mention in the earlier fourteenth-century ordinances of the guild of St James, the religious fraternity which was responsible, among other things, for much personal support, and which features so frequently in the craft's fifteenth-century accounts. Since the members often met in secret, they were regarded by the government of the day as clandestine societies and, as such, might be politically suspect. It therefore may have seemed wiser not to draw attention in the ordinances to this religious fraternity.

THE DEVELOPMENT OF THE CRAFT 1356–1462

Despite being recognised as a craft with its own ordinances, the pinners remained among the humblest members of the metal-work trades. As an artisan mystery they cut little ice in City affairs, dominated as these were by the merchants and leading craft companies. Individual pinners could be obstreperous however. In December 1371, in the mayor's court, John atte Hill, a pinner, alongside Simon Chikesond and John White, a furbour, went to prison 'for breaking a sequestration of the King's tallage', one of a number of such protests in the city at that time.[14] The pinners were to a considerable extent dependent on the patronage of those larger companies which had a professional interest in the supply of pins: notably the tailors, mercers and later the haberdashers who traded wholesale on a national scale.[15]

In the 1370s the rivalries between different crafts came to a head and in 1376 it was decided that election to the Common Council should be by the crafts rather than the traditional wards. The Pinners, along with an impressive array of metal workers, armourers, cutlers, lorimers, pewterers, plumbers, smiths and spurriers, sent representatives to the Common Council in the years 1376–81.[16] The champion of the lesser crafts was the

14. *CPMR 1364–81*, p. 135.
15. Matthew Davies, *The Merchant Tailors' Company of London: Court Minutes 1486–1493* (Stamford, 2000); Anne Sutton, *The Mercery of London: Trade, Goods and People, 1130–1578* (Aldershot, 2005); Ian Archer, *The History of the Haberdashers' Company* (Chichester, 1991).
16. Caroline M. Barron, *London in the Later Middle Ages: Government and People* (Oxford, 2004), p. 220.

draper, John of Northampton. When he was superseded as mayor by Nicholas Brembre in 1383, rioting followed among John's supporters. It is not, therefore, surprising to find a pinner, John Dawntre, a warden in 1378, mainprised in the sum of £100 for his future good behaviour and, by implication that of his fellow members, nor to read the names of cutlers and armourers who were similarly constrained.[17]

Only one pinner was arraigned for participation in the Peasants' Revolt of 1381, a William Bylneye of Coleman Street, and, in January 1389, Margery Bromhill, widow of Hugh, a pinner, was granted a pardon 'for all offences entailing penalty of life, limb or forfeiture, between 1 October 1382 and 31 May 1388...'. This pardon presumably refers to participation in the events following the succession of Nicholas Brembre to the mayoralty and the departure of John Northampton.[18] From then on, the pinners appear to have eschewed political affiliations and concentrated on more immediate and mundane concerns. Their appearances in the mayor's court thereafter were mainly confined to matters of apprenticeship, fraud and service as mainpernors for friends and neighbours. An unusual case involving a pinner in 1377 occurred when "Robert Cheyndut was committed to prison for having undertaken to cure Walter, son of John del Hull, pinner, of a malady in his left leg, whereby owing to lack of care, the patient was in danger of losing his leg...". The plaintiff was awarded 50s. in damages[19]

The weakness of all craft ordinances was that the craft could not control or restrict wholesale trade in its products. Judicious wardens, in company with city officers, could search for clandestine retailers and manufacturers within the walls but they could not prevent wealthy merchants from dealing in large quantities on the home or foreign markets. As already shown, the pinners relied for their profits on trades and crafts which used pins in their daily work, notably the tailors and mercers. It was but a step for such men, whose businesses involved them in transactions, at both manufacturing and mercantile levels, to start selling pins on their own account. It was a phenomenon that affected many craftsmen in many trades. Even pinners trespassed into other crafts: John Godefray, was twice brought before the mayor by the Hurers (cap-makers) , in 1391 and 1394, for selling false 'caps' as a sideline and was fined.[20]

Later, the haberdashers surpassed all comers in the distribution of a wide range of goods throughout the country, including pins, through travelling chapmen and fairs. According to Chaucer, moreover, even the odd friar

17. *CPMR 1381–1412*, p. 63; for the will of John Dawntre (**70**).
18. *CPMR 1364–81*, p. 289. In the writ to the mayor, the king wished to be certified as to whether Margery, widow of Hugh Bromhill, pinner, was one of the citizens of the city, *CPMR 1381–1413*, p. 151.
19. *CPMR 1364–81*, p. 236; for the will of John atte Hill (**69**).
20. *LBH*, pp. 366, 403.

was known to use pins as petty bribes.[21] At wholesale level, there was a thin line between the pinner and the haberdasher, but a very large one when it came to influence and prestige in the city. In the fifteenth century, two prosperous pinners bowed to the inevitable and, with mayoral approval, switched their allegiances to the haberdashers: Richard Lyon in 1432 and Thomas Byset in 1449.[22] Earlier still, in 1401, William de Coventre had declared for the mercers on the same grounds.[23] In this way these three men became eligible for city office, should it come in their direction, but it deprived the pinners of the support and interest which such men could have brought to the craft, including legacies of money and real estate. Without such help, as time was to prove, it could be difficult for a craft to survive in hard times

The mystery emerged as an embattled group in 1425 when, together with the wiredrawers and cardmakers, they came before the mayor to lodge complaints against one another. Allied trades though they were, each complained that 'within the last six or seven years some freemen of the mystery of Pynners had employed and coloured strange Wirdrawers and Cardemakers, therefore depriving the Irenwirdrawers and Cardemakers of their livelihood; also that certain freemen of the said mystery of Irenwirdrawers and Cardemakers had employed and coloured foreign Pynners, whereby many free Pynners were deprived of their livelihood, and thus dissension had oftentimes arisen.' It was a classic dispute of that period. Such invasions of the rights of other crafts were all too common when so many 'specialist' tradesmen all shared similar skills. The dispute was resolved, as in other cases, by specific prohibition in the ordinances of each mystery, forbidding members to employ workmen of the other crafts or to practise those crafts themselves.[24]

The responsibility for carrying out searches of workshops to ensure good workmanship was fraught with problems. As already indicated, where two or more trades formed one company, the expertise of the officers involved could be called into question if they were inspecting a craft other than their own. It was, moreover, an expensive exercise because the wardens of the mystery needed the legal support of a mayor's sergeant to carry it out and payment was required for his services.

21. His tipet was ay farsed ful of knyves
And pinnes, for to yeven faire wyves
Geoffrey Chaucer, *Canterbury Tales*, Prologue lines 233–234
22. *LBK*, pp. 144, 327.
23. *LBI*, p. 15. See Jean M. Imray, ' "Les Bones Gentes de la Mercerye de Londres": a study of the membership of the Medieval Mercers' Company', in A. E. J. Hollaender and William Kellaway eds., *Studies in London History presented to Philip Edmund Jones* (London, 1970), pp. 155–178, esp. pp. 165–6; also Anne F. Sutton, *A Merchant Family of Coventry, London and Calais: The Tates, c.1450–1515* (London, 1998), p. 11
24. *LBK*, pp. 42–43

In 1452 the pinners once more appeared before the mayor to protest strongly concerning the practices of his own officers. They pointed out that, in the past, where an official search was carried out by the mystery, it had been customary, when culprits were fined, for the Guildhall to retain half of the money and for the craft to take the rest. In a recent case however, in which a pinner, named John Bultell, had committed an offence normally punishable by a fine of 40 shillings, the chamberlain had let him go on payment of a fine of 6s. 8d. and had refused to give the craft's wardens anything 'for all her said labour and costes'. They stressed that they were asking for the right 'to take for their laboure as Wardeins of other Craftes of this Citee haven and they shall pray to God for you'. Their prayers prevailed and their petition was granted.[25]

Most pinners were comparatively poor men. It is perhaps surprising that more were not tempted into dishonesty than would seem to have been the case. In 1449, however, William Taylour allowed himself to become involved in a curious fraud. He was employed to deliver a forged document to a pewterer, John Kinsale. He had agreed 'to seal the deed as though it had been sealed by the said John Kinsale and to pass himself off as John Kinsale...'. The prime mover in the fraud was a William Halman, who later confessed his guilt and was sentenced to stand in the pillory. William Taylour, the pinner, also confessed his part in the deception 'and said that he had received in payment from the said William Halman a shoulder of mutton, a gallon of ale and 20 pence'.[26]

Two master pinners, at the other end of the scale, ran into problems over apprentices. The first arose over the death of the master himself, Laurence Proute. Young Geoffrey Prany, of Livermere in Suffolk, complained in the mayor's court in 1444, that he had been apprenticed for ten years to Laurence Proute, pinner, whose widow and executrix Agnes had remarried to Thomas Holgill gentleman 'and that the said Agnes kept no shop and had not instructed or provided for him wherefore he prayed to be exonerated from his apprenticeship': which he duly was.[27] The other case revealed how vulnerable an apprentice could be if placed with a harsh master. Thomas Duffield, son of a London cordwainer, had been apprenticed to a pinner, Thomas Boges, for eight years. In 1447, he was excused from the rest of his apprenticeship on the ground that his master had not instructed him in his trade, and had 'chastised him horribly'.[28]

A notable feature of the later audit book is the expenditure by the Pinners on the upkeep of the then newly-acquired hall. It appears that, as early as 1443, the Pinners were renting a property from the Merchant Taylors' Company. An entry in the court minutes of the Merchant Taylors'

25. *LBK*, pp. 344–45
26. 26 February 1449, *CPMR 1437–57*, p. 112
27. *CPMR 1437–57*, pp. 69–70.
28. *CPMR 1437–57*, p. 95.

Company in 1443–4 recorded money spent on repairs to the 'pynners hous', at that time located in Friday Street. Since the craft was no longer renting this property in 1462, it must have been relinquished at some time before then, perhaps reflecting the toll taken on the industry by the increase of foreign imports following the end of the Hundred Years' War in 1453.[29]

THE PINNERS' CRAFT IN LONDON 1462–98

The end of the war with France had brought decline in some trades, notably the wool industry, and taxation was high. But the impact on towns was variable. Some towns declined sharply at this period but others, such as Westminster, prospered.[30] This was not always a result of the war but reflected industrial and market changes, in particular, the switch from the wholesale export of wool to the manufacture of woollen cloth. For the pinners, the increase of foreign imports represented a serious threat. Unfortunately for them, their interests ran counter to those of the wholesale merchants', many of whom imported and distributed these manufactured goods, and also to those of the king, who welcomed the customs duties paid on such imported goods.

In 1462 the Cutlers Company headed a deputation to the new king, Edward IV, on behalf of a number of small traders, including the pinners, seeking a ban on the foreign imports which, they claimed, menaced their livelihoods. For the time being their prayer was granted in a statute, the so-called 'Charter' of 1463. Reassured by this, the Pinners proceeded to put their affairs in order and to conduct their business in the manner of a city company, a status to which they, like many other humble associations, aspired.[31]

As a first step, they ordered a scribe to have made a copy of the prized 'Charter', referred to as 'our Exemplification' (i.e. of the 1463 Parliamentary Statute), as a safeguard against any future encroachments upon it by forgetful authorities (**2**). In the absence of a hall of their own, they deposited the document in the Girdlers' Hall for safekeeping. The next step was to buy parchment and a calendar which were bound together as a book in which the craft would inscribe its ordinances, a copy of the 'Charter' and enter the wardens' biennial statements of account. This record was kept, with varying efficiency, for nearly fifty years and it is this manuscript which is edited here.

29. GL, Merchant Taylors' Company, Wardens' Accounts, 1398–1445, fol. 380v.
30. J. Hatcher, 'The Great Slump of the Mid-Fifteenth Century', in R. Britnell and J. Hatcher eds., *Progress and Problems in Medieval England: Essays in Honour of Edward Miller* (Cambridge, 1996), pp. 237–72; Gervase Rosser, 'The essence of medieval urban communities: The vill of Westminster 1200–1540', in Richard Holt and Gervase Rosser eds., *The English Medieval Town: A Reader in English Urban History 1200–1540* (Harlow, 1990), pp. 216–38.
31. 1463, 3 Edward IV c.4, *SR*, pp. 396–98.

Its pages reveal, not only the erratic course of a very humble craft, but also, in some instances, the uncertain fortunes of individual members. It also revealed that, like many other crafts, the brotherhood of pinners was both a religious and craft association. In the first two years of this record (1462–4), the craft spent nearly 12% of its funds in its capacity as the Fraternity of St James. Its membership was open to all workmen, as well as the masters and their wives. It was this organisation which ensured the social cohesion and support of the craft. Through it, trental masses were said for the souls of members on their deaths and, annually, for the welfare of all past and present members of the craft. These masses were celebrated at the Whitefriars at a cost of 2s 6d on each occasion. The brethren also mounted candles there on the feast of St James, 25 July, as well as at the nearby Augustinian hospital of Elsyng Spital and at the hospital of St James at Westminster. Large amounts of money were paid to the waxchandler each year for the supply of costly candles and the sexton at Elsyng Spital received a regular payment for scouring the sconce there. As members came and went, a scribe or painter was paid to keep the membership 'tables' up to date. These were kept at Elsyng Spital. Overall, this was quite a widely spread outlay of charitable donations for a not very prosperous craft.[32]

By their own standards however, and despite their valid complaints against foreign competition, the pinners were comparatively thriving at this time. Though never large, there were probably about sixteen master craftsmen in 1462. The umper and his two wardens opened the book with immediate receipts of £5 5s. 6d. and, after paying out £10 5s. 4d. during their two years of office, they handed on £18 0s. 6d. to their successors in 1464.[33] And this was despite a number of extraordinary expenses, totalling £2 6s. 8d., the sum which the Pinners paid towards the Cutlers' petition. Such a balance compares favourably with many entries in the accounts of their contemporaries, the Carpenters, which was a well established craft with many more members.[34]

As might be expected, 88% of their total outgoings were disbursed on running the craft itself. Some of this money was spent on their civic duties. For however humble their craft, the masters were, by definition, freemen of the city of London, a privileged status, which required their presence annually, when first the sheriffs, and then the mayor, after their election, travelled to Westminster to present themselves to the king. City custom demanded that the wardens of each company took part in this ceremony in liveries provided at their own expense. Evidently a convivial occasion, it is

32. For accounts of Elsyng Spital and the Hospital of St James, see Caroline M. Barron and Matthew Davies, eds., *The Religious Houses of London and Middlesex* (London, 2007), pp. 165–68; 177–181.
33. The term 'umper' describes the senior warden who, presumably, acted as the senior arbitrator in the affairs of the craft.
34. Marsh, ed., *Records of...Company of Carpenters*, vol. 2 passim .

interesting to find in the first account, but never again, a payment of 16d., laid out on a breakfast for those not of the livery who had been excluded from the mayor's dinner. Providing liveries for participants at official events was another charge on the Pinners' resources. In 1465, the brethren paid 15s. for woollen cloth 'ayenst the quenes coronation'(**8**); and in the 1468–70 account 3½d. was paid 'for drinking at St. Katherine's when the king came up by water', and 15s. for five yards of cloth when King Edward returned from the north of England (**13**).

The payments made by the craft for carrying out obligatory searches make clear the burden this laid upon small trades. Among the payments, it is interesting to find references to searches carried out beyond the city's jurisdiction: at the fair of Stourbridge, for example, on behalf of the wiredrawers, and again in the same period (1462–4) at Salisbury (**4**).

Nor were these the only financial calls on the craft. Once an apprentice had completed his term of service, he could, on payment of 3s. 4d., be registered as a brother of the fraternity and was qualified to work as a skilled journeyman. He was also entitled to become a freeman of the City, if and when he could raise the entry fee. Before taking this step, it was usual to spend a few years as a journeyman. This group of young men was sometimes referred to as the 'bachelors', a practice which explains the entry, against a donation, 'from the young men of the craft' (**3**).[35] Understandably, the freedom of the city was much coveted and many journeymen undoubtedly never attained it. Without it however no man, whatever his skill, could set up his own shop, employ journeymen or take on apprentices. A number of entries in the accounts indicate that, like other crafts, the pinners had a type of loan scheme to enable men to take up the freedom. The money was paid back in instalments of 8d. a week, paid each Saturday. Each loan was covered by a bond, for which legal fees were incurred (**7**).

Other payments were directed to maintaining the dignity of the fraternity. By 1462, the craft had a beadle, that indispensable factotum of any self-respecting mystery. Richard Quycke's wages were 6s. 8d. *p.a.* and a distinctive 'half hood' was provided for him, at a cost of 5s. (**4**) On his death, as a brother of the fraternity, the craft paid for a mass to be sung for his soul (**51**).

The number of master-craftsmen at any one time must always have been small. The overall numbers of the fraternity - as distinct from the craft - are difficult to gauge. Women, including all the wives, could and did join the fraternity but were not accepted as members of the craft itself. The purchase of five dozen trenchers in 1462 sounds ambitious (**4**). Scrutiny of the accounts however, shows that, in the twenty years between 1462 and 1482, there were thirty admissions to the fraternity: sixteen men, a

35. On young men and 'bachelors' in city companies, see Caroline M. Barron, *London in the Later Middle Ages* (Oxford, 2004), pp. 211–14.

single woman and thirteen wives. If the names of at least seven wardens and their wives are added, and the husbands of the newly-admitted wives, the total membership comes to just over thirty and there were undoubtedly a number of others, particularly journeymen, who do not appear in the records. In this way, it can be seen that a total of sixty people might well have attended the annual feast of St James. Only men could attend business meetings, at which their presence was compulsory, with a fine for unexplained absence. There is evidence of some unrest among older members at this time, perhaps reflecting a recent tightening up of regulations. In the first account, several members are fined for non-attendance at the audit and for a number of offences against the ordinances such as employing children who were not apprenticed as well as poaching other members' workmen (**6**).

The earlier fourteenth-century ordinances had specified that women could only practise the trade if they were the wives or daughters of a member of the craft. In later days, however, the names of a few unidentifiable women do appear in the lists, paying the fees to become full members of the craft. Some of these would almost certainly be 'forins' who had learnt their skills outside the city and now presented themselves as competent artificers. There is no record of a girl being apprenticed as a pinner, but presumably those who did work in the trade had learnt their skills in their fathers' and husbands' workshops. Exceptionally, a Margaret Hall paid 10s. in 1477–81 for admission as a freewoman and at the same time one Isabell Goor paid 10d. quarterage (**22**). On marriage, all the brethren appear to have paid the entrance fee of 20d. to make their wives sisters of St James. This entitled them to attend the fraternity's social gatherings and paid for a trental mass, at the Whitefriars, in the event of their deaths.

One or two widows may have paid the full membership fee of 3s. 4d. on the deaths of their husbands, which suggests their intention of keeping up the workshop, and training the apprentices, on their own account. There is insufficient evidence to prove this either way, though the legal case brought by an apprentice in 1444, against a widow, Agnes Proute, for failing to provide instruction for him, might imply that this was accepted practice. With the influx of 'forin' workers 'in Robert Ettell's time,' in about 1498, four workwomen were admitted: Margaret Exnyng, Margaret Golde, Margaret Crayford and Katherine Smyth (**56**).

Their surviving wills reveal some of the areas in which pinners lived in London. The parishes of twenty-six pinners ranging in date from 1395 to 1558 are known.[36] All but three of these pinners lived in a tight cluster of parishes in the north-west corner of the city and stretching out into the western suburbs. Six of the pinners lived in the parish of St Bride in Fleet

36. See Appendix 1

Street.[37] One of the pinners who lived in Fleet Street, Richard Hughis, shortly before his death in 1468, had been summoned to appear before the Court of Common Pleas for arrears of rent on his workshop. The court record provides the only known description of a pinner's working premises. It lay in the parish of St Bride and consisted of a shop made 'sidewise' by the street situated next to Fleet Bridge, above the water there.[38]

With a satisfactory membership and an unspecified number of apprentices, 1462 was the high-water mark of the craft. There was money to pay for a beadle and his hood, civic journeys to Westminster, and for new liveries for the wardens who accompanied royal ridings, alongside other crafts and companies. At this point, the umpers and wardens might well have dreamed of becoming a fully-fledged city company, with a hall of their own and all the dignities which went with such a position.

In 1462, the Pinners had no premises of their own, whatever premises they may have been able to rent from the Taylors earlier in the century. When the new book opened, they were holding their biennial audit and elections in the Girdlers' Hall, which they hired for 2s. a time. They provided their own table linen on these occasions, which periodically cost 12d. for laundering, and doubtless made use of the five dozen wooden trenchers, which they had bought in 1462, at a cost of 15d. In the absence of a permanent base, storage was an obvious problem. In the first year, the brethren laid out 2s. for 'a little new cheste for our Crafte'. The treasured 'exemplification' of the 1462 ordinance had to be deposited in the Cutlers' Hall for safe-keeping (**4**).[39]

They were not alone in such aspirations. The fifteenth century witnessed the acquisition, extension and building of many such halls. The Carpenters, for example, began work on theirs in 1438 and were still working on it twenty years later. Less pretentious crafts, such as the Bowyers, were also providing themselves with such premises in the 1460s. By 1470, moreover, the Pinners had moved out of the Girdlers' Hall. The account for 1470 had to be presented in the brewhouse at the sign of the Rose, in the Old Jewry (**13**). Though doubtless convivial, this venue was hardly consonant with the pride of the fraternity. In 1472, they assembled in the Armourers' Hall, for which they paid a rent of 3s. 4d. that year and subsequently 10s. for three further years (**15, 17**).[40] By 1481 they had made the decision to lease a hall in Adel Street, off Wood Street in Cripplegate ward, from Thomas

37. St Bride (6); St Martin Pomeroy (3); St Peter Westchepe (2); St Mary Magdalen (2); St Sepulchre (2); St Michael Wood Street (2); St Matthew Friday Street (3); and one each in the parishes of St Lawrence Jewry, St Botolph Aldersgate, St Alban Wood Street, St Magnus, St Katherine Christchurch and St Mary Somerset.
38. TNA CP 40/825 rot. 424 (Plea Rolls of the Court of Common Pleas).
39. The Girdlers' Hall was in what is now Basinghall Street, the Cutlers' Hall was in La Riole.
40. The Armourers' Hall was at the corner of London Wall and Coleman Street.

Payne, a carpenter who rented it from the Taylors' Company, for 20s. *p.a.* (**22, 26**). The umper and wardens rendered their first account in the new building in November 1481, doubtless with much rejoicing (**24**).[41]

Unfortunately, their pleasure was to be short-lived. In no time they were paying heavily for their high aspirations. The indentures for renting the hall cost 2s. 4d., but this was only the beginning. Whether the building was dilapidated, or whether the Pinners sought to improve and extend it, is not known. What is certain is that, no sooner had they moved in, than they had to call the builders in at much expense (**23, 26, 29, 32**). Their hall was evidently a timber and daub construction. There are entries in the accounts of the payment of 15s. 'to the Carpynter for his wages' and 25s. 'to the Dawber and his man', not to mention the purchase, for £2 12s. 10d., of laths, boards, loam, sand, gravel, bricks, lime, masonry, nails and iron work. That done, there was 3s. 4d. to pay for carting away the rubbish, 31s.1d. 'for steynyng of the hallyng', 18d. for red lead and 7½d. for 'moty' (a kind of pigment). Furnishing and finishing involved 7d. for coal, 4s. for a table and two trestles, 16d. for four forms, 2s. 2d. for 'mattes in the hall and parlour' and 7d. for a lock. Under the circumstances, it is remarkable that the wardens had a balance of £7 2s. 6d. at the next audit (**24**).

Nor was this the end of the story. More work on the building had to be done in the next two years and in most years thereafter. The overall balance had dropped to £5 12s. 5d. in 1483. By 1487, however, it had returned to £6 1s. 9½d. On the back of this last account is an undated inventory of the contents of the hall, written in an unpractised hand, perhaps that of one of the pinners. It is a meagre record of linen, dishes and platters, banners and a pall. Since there is no mention of furniture, not even the trestle tables and stools, this list may have been made for a specific purpose and therefore incomplete (**31**).

There were further repairs to the hall in 1490, but the craft may well have hoped that its outlay was about to pay off, when the wardens of the Daubers paid the Pinners 16d. for the use of their hall for a supper (**34**). But both finances and accounts showed a sharp decline from then on and the balance handed to the new wardens in 1491 was reduced to £3 9s. 10d. Worse was to come, with yet another visitation of epidemic disease in the early 1490s. There remained a number of unpaid debts to the craft and in 1496 the account showed that £2 4s. 10d. was still owed by members, probably quite legitimately under bonds, though there is no record of these (**39**). The fact remained, the new wardens started their term with assets of £1 6s. 4d. Similar small balances had featured in the accounts of the more prosperous Carpenters, particularly when building operations were in full spate. The Carpenters had even been driven to pawning some

41. In the accounts for 1479–80, it was recorded that Thomas Payne, a carpenter, paid rent to the Taylors' Company for the 'hall used by the pinners', GL, Merchant Taylors' Company, Wardens' Accounts 1469–1484, fol. 380v.

of their plate and 'kishions' to the goldsmiths in 1458. The difference between the two crafts, however, was that, by 1442 the Carpenters had acquired 'tenametys' which yielded rent. This additional income was a permanent reinforcement, however bad the cash balance looked.[42] It was a resource unlikely ever to come the way of the pinners when their wealthiest members tended to migrate to major companies.

The costs of the hall were probably not the only cause of the disastrous slump in their fortunes. The circumstances surrounding the death of Thomas Tarte, some time between 1475 and 1477, may throw further light on the situation. Admitted to the brotherhood in 1462, with his wife, he may have been a foreign workman, trained outside the city, who, after due consideration, had been accepted into the craft. He rose rapidly and became a warden in 1466, and again in 1475. He died in office owing the craft £4 under a bond, the money with which he had been vested when elected a warden. Unusually, the craft distrained his property to recover the money. It returned gradually. Katherine Hill, perhaps a married daughter, held 18s. 5d. worth of his goods in 1477 and subsequently paid over £1 5s.11d. Later still, she paid in 15s. 3d. 'for Tartes goods' which at least redeemed a little over half of the missing capital, but it also cost the craft 8d. for carting the goods away and another 3s. 4d. 'for the man that laboured for Tartes goods'; not to mention fees paid at the Guildhall (**19, 21, 23**).

The case is of interest since it was the one occasion on which the wardens were prepared to take such drastic action. When Edmund Legge, another former warden, died, c.1472–5, during his term of office, he also owed £4 under a legal obligation, of which only £1 10s. was paid back, some time after 1479 (**21, 22**). The facts relating to this man are somewhat mysterious. Evidently one of the leading men of the craft, he served as warden twice: in 1466–8 and 1472–5. He also acted, as did a number of other pinners , as the recipient of gifts of goods and chattels enrolled among the records of the mayor's court. In September 1469, he was one of four recipients for William Smyth, a hatter, and two months later, he was one of three men who accepted the same role for John Lamberd, a girdler.[43] Legge was therefore familiar with this legal agreement and it is not surprising to find that he had himself engaged in financial transactions of this kind (often used as a means of obtaining short-term credit) with another pinner, John Ronell (**91**).[44]

42. 1438, Received 'off the Tenauntrye for the year, 26s 8d.'; 1458 the craft received 'of the tenantys in the allmes housys' 7s. 11d. Marsh, ed., *Records of...Company of Carpenters*, pp. 1, 27
43. *CPMR 1458–82*, pp. 162, 163; for the significance of these gifts, see *CPMR 1437–57,* pp. xxii-xxviii.
44. As early as 1439, John Edrych, pinner, had conveyed all his goods and chattels to Henry Farnby, brewer and Thomas Plot, leatherseller, perhaps to avoid a distraint of goods: he took the same action again in 1447. When Edrych drew up his will, he made Thomas Plot his principal executor (**84**). On other occasions pinners acted as feoffees in uses. It would appear that Edmund Legge undertook the role of trustee on a number of occasions, see *CCR 1468–76,* nos. 161, 297, 390, 436, 813, and also the will of John Ronell (**91**).

On the other hand, when John Plays died while serving as umper between 1481–3, his widow immediately paid back the £3 5s. 10d. he then owed (**24, 25**). Most of the loans to members were probably repaid. As already shown, men who had borrowed to become freemen met their debts in weekly instalments, usually of 8d. at a time. It is possible nonetheless that the craft may have overreached itself in making such advances given that it did not possess any property to provide financial security.

Another element in the situation was reflected in the new petition of many small crafts, including the Pinners, to Richard III on his accession in 1483. This plea echoed that of 1462, in its request for an embargo on foreign imports and seemingly with as little long-term effect.[45] It was a forlorn hope since, as before, they were up against the conflict of interest between local craftsmen and wholesale merchant importers.

The umper and wardens of 1495 were forced to recognise that the fraternity as it stood was no longer viable. It was a common enough situation among small crafts. In 1479, the wiredrawers had been forced to take the step of amalgamating with the chapemakers, to become the craft of wiremongers, a fairly frequent expedient among small crafts, faced with foreign competition and rising unemployment at home. Unwin suggested that the Pinners' undoing was their 'fatal decision' to have a hall. Certainly it cost them a great deal but their accounts indicate that their finances were declining even before that. From their standpoint, the hall might have represented a good investment, to be rented out and thus to yield income. There were other forces at work, outside the craft itself, which worked against the pinners, alongside many other small trades. Alien competition, against which they had inveighed in 1462, continued to increase. The records of the London petty custom reveal that, in the single year of 1481, huge cargoes of pins were coming into the ports from overseas.[46] Hence the petition to Richard III in which protection against foreign imports was again sought.

The records of many crafts in the 1490s show a remarkable increase in the numbers of 'forin' workmen joining the trade and the men of the mysteries were petitioning the mayor and aldermen for the tightening up of regulations governing the admission of such workmen. What none of them clearly could understand was the cheapness of the goods from abroad, and in some cases, their high quality, particularly those from the Low Countries.[47] They appear

45. 1483, 1 Richard III c.12, *SR*, vol. 2, pp. 495–96. For the background to this petition and statute, see Anne F. Sutton and L. Visser-Fuchs, *Richard III's Books: Ideals and Reality in the Life and Library of a Medieval Prince* (Stroud, 1997), pp. 244–246.
46. H.S. Cobb ed., *The Overseas Trade of London: Exchequer Customs Accounts 1480–1* (London Record Society, 1990), s.v. 'pins' in index. 13 November 1481, a ship came into the post of London with a cargo of Flemish manufactured good including 8,000 pins, see no. 25.
47. See complaint from the Glovers, 12 December 1482, *LBL*, p. 203; complaint from the Fullers, 27 March 1487, *LBL*, p. 242; complaint from the Skinners, 21 May 1493, *LBL*, p. 295.

to have been unaware of, or refused to acknowledge, the technical developments in Europe which made these improvements possible, although Osmund steel from Sweden, the basis for hard steel wire, the pinners' basic material, was being imported into England in the fifteenth century.[48]

Overall, the craft was probably a victim of its own over-regulated practices. Manufacturing processes prescribed by the craft itself and enforced by the wardens inhibited new methods of working and stifled technical innovation at source. The series of infectious epidemics at this period may also have contributed to the pinners' difficulties. John Plays, while serving as umper 1481–3, could well have died of such illness.

In 1495, the new wardens, William Parker, Robert Ettell and Robert Chenwyth took office with a total of only £1 6s 4d. in the box. They now had the sad task of winding up the Pinners' affairs and negotiating the amalgamation of their craft with the Wiremongers, their suppliers. Even this process proved expensive. Nearly £1 10s. of the outgoings for 1498 went on 'the cost of the plea betwyxte the pynners and the wyremongers' (**41**). Most of the money went on the drafting of pleas and legal documents, not to mention the expenses incurred in entertaining the mayor and various legal worthies. The Pinners paid 20d. for the enrolment of the ordinances of the craft, in its new name of Wiresellers, in the city's Letter Book L (**41**).[49] Not surprisingly, only 7s. 6½d. was left in the common box at the end of 1497. The number of pinners on roll at the time appears to have been fourteen in all.

It must have been a sad and worrying time. There is no reason to suppose negligence on the part of John Wekys himself, a warden during the final years 1491–1495, but the successive deaths of umpers and wardens over the years led to some loss of capital to the craft. It remains a mystery why John Wekys never held office again after 1495 although he did not die until 1518 (**96**). Perhaps the former pinners did hold him responsible to some extent for the collapse of the craft. It is also possible that he may have been so disheartened that he asked to be excused further service. Given the costs of the whole transaction, it is also possible that he was himself financially embarrassed by the need to subsidise the craft at this period, but he was certainly still in business at the time of his death.

THE WIRESELLERS 1498–1511

However common the amalgamation of crafts might be, for the participants such amalgamations inevitably brought fundamental changes. The Wiremongers had been through the process fairly recently in 1479, when

48. Geddes, 'Iron' in Blair and Ramsay eds., *English Medieval Industries*, pp. 167–88, esp. p. 168, and W.R. Childs, 'England's iron trade in the Fifteenth Century', *EcHR*, 34 (1981).
49. *LBL*, pp. 319–320; see **65**, **66**.

they combined with the Chapemakers, another union forced on both parties by economic necessity.[50] On that occasion, however, there was no problem about their patron saint and fraternity. Their new ordinances of 1481 had reaffirmed their continued adherence to the feast day of St Clement the Pope (23 November): ' that it be kept and halowed as it is kept and halowed among other craftes of the same citee that in their werk occupie fire and water in eschewyng the hurtes that myght come thereby...'[51]. In espousing St James, the Pinners appear to have deviated from the usual affiliation of the many other metal workers in the city. It is possible that the craft may originally have met together in the hospital dedicated to St James at Westminster. They had now to agree to accept St Clement, along with their new identity as Wiresellers, although the Pinners seem to have kept some tokens of their old allegiance. In the account for 1497–99 the payment of 10s. is recorded 'for a banner of the Assumption of Our Lady and St Clement with anchors and scallop shells'. Presumably, the scallop shells were a residual reference to their association with St James. In the same account 15s. was also spent on an image of St Clement, and a further 1d. for wax and resin for the image (**47**). A special subscription for the banner and the image raised 5s. 10d. towards the cost (**53**).

Since the Wiredrawers do not appear to have had a hall, the Pinners' Hall in Adel Street was retained, though it still occasioned insatiable demands for repairs, and, on at least one occasion, in 1504, they had to move out into 'our hall in the Greyfriars', at a rent of 20d. for the year (**45, 58**).

The real drain on the new craft's resources, however, was a law suit between the brethren and a man called Thomas Hill, conducted in the Commissary Court between 1497 to 1499. To meet the costs initially, thirty-one members subscribed £1 5s.11d. between them in varying amounts. This is the first complete list of the craft: fourteen of the men so named are identifiable as former pinners (**43**). The case against Thomas Hill continued its laborious course. Expenses amounted to 19s. 6d. in the first year and further large sums were paid out in 1499, for which there were more levies. Finally, the Court ordained that each of the parties should pay in 40s., a sum raised by yet another subscription (**44, 51**).

From the beginning, money had to be raised by extraordinary measures. As already indicated, with the common box virtually empty and legal expenses mounting, the Wiresellers resorted to 'ales'. Entry fees were clearly graded to the members' means. Even the food and candles for the annual Saint's day feast had to be funded in this way (**52**).

The form of these later accounts, if such they can be called, varied at this time, evidently depending on the priorities of the moment; even their dating is sometimes haphazard. Indeed they might more often be described

50. *LBL*, p. 168
51. *LBL*, pp. 185–186

as memoranda, rather than accounts. The period 1499–1504 is characterised by a number of different listings. One of the most interesting, dated 1497–99 lists the names of twenty-four 'foreigners' who paid fines to be allowed to work in the city (**56**). One of these was, John Myryell, who paid 6s. 8d. for his freedom. Of the remaining twenty-three people, four women each paid 20d. to be admitted as workwomen and eighteen men paid the same sum to become workmen. One man, however, was charged 2s. as part payment of his fine to be admitted as a workman.

However insecure their finances, the craft continued to hire two barges each year to accompany first the sheriffs and then the mayor to Westminster, taking their place as a recognised craft of the city. In 1504, they spent 5s. 1d. on the erection of a scaffold for the entry of Prince Arthur and Catherine of Aragon, for which a small group of senior men provided the money (**58, 59**). Routine payments continued until 1511, when Robert Cadman, John Wright and John Strode presented their account, the last one recorded. They delivered into the common box, on this occasion, 34s., and they noted that there was 'remaining to the craft' and the company in quarterage 30s. (**64**).

There are no further entries. The Wiresellers appear to have been absorbed into the Girdlers, although it is not clear when this happened.[52] Certainly, much later, in the reign of Elizabeth, the Pinners were to break away from the Girdlers to become an independent craft once more. But in 1511, their book of records was closed. It remains, however muddled and confused in places, a valuable insight into the realities of life for an artisan craft, struggling for survival, like many others of their kind, against economic forces and rivalries which they were not in a position to withstand. Clinging to the craft processes and traditions of an earlier period, the Pinners were doubtless bewildered to find that their skills, in no way eroded, were no longer valued as they had been, and they were forced to accept the unwelcome influx of imported goods.

PHYSICAL DESCRIPTION OF THE BOOK AND ITS ARRANGEMENT

The first audit reported the costs of making the new book in detail: 2s. 5d. for thirteen skins of parchment, 10d. for a rubricated calendar and 12d. for binding, and for clasps that have now gone (**4**). When the volume was bound at some later date the pages were cropped to fit the new covers. The volume was rebound in 1976. As it now stands, the seventy-one pages measure 7 inches by 9½ inches. The small, six-folio rubricated calendar of saints' days was added to the front of the volume when it was first

52. Unwin, p. 306; Barker argues that the wiresellers did not pass under the aegis of the Girdlers until 1527, when loans had begun to be levied from the crafts, T.C.Barker, *The Girdlers' Company: A Second History* (London, 1957), p. 50; Reps, vol.vii, f. 263.

compiled in the fifteenth century. The pages were re-numbered in ink at a later date and more consistent numbering in pencil has been added in modern times.

It is rarely possible to pinpoint the exact dates of events referred to in the book, although the sequence of accounts is unbroken. Royal events can sometimes be identified and the deaths of individual pinners can be reasonably assigned if they left wills, particularly in the case of probated wills. The preparation of these accounts clearly depended on some other accounting records, such as bills, which are sometimes referred to in the text, but none has survived.[53] Like other crafts, the Pinners were by their ordinances required to report the names of their new officers at Guildhall, but, to judge from the evidence of the City's Letter Books, they did so only sporadically, or at least the names of the new officers were only sporadically recorded. A list of the names of the umpers and wardens recorded, both in the Letter Books and in the accounts, is given in Appendix 2. The Pinners appear to have confined themselves to three officers at a time: an umper and two wardens, and the records show that this custom was substantially unchanged during this period.

EDITORIAL METHOD

The aim throughout has been to produce a modern English version of the manuscript. Some attempt has been made to render proper names consistently. Variant names will be found in the index.

For easy reference the text has been broken into numbered paragraphs where natural breaks in the text emerge and there are several in each biennial account. On occasion modern punctuation has been added to clarify the sense of an entry. Where words have obviously been omitted, these have been inserted, in square brackets, as have modern variants of archaic words. Latin words are given as cited but, where possible, with standard contractions expanded. Illegible or missing words are indicated with omission marks.

Most of the wills calendared at the end of the main text, were written in Latin. These wills have been rephrased in modern English and set out in paragraphs in order to be more easily understood. For the sake of convenience, each will has been transcribed with paragraph numbers, but these are not in the originals. Similarly, in the interest of reducing formulaic repetition, some of the original preamble has been omitted: the opening phrase of the last will and testament, namely 'In the name of God, Amen', and the full details of regnal years and titles. Although some of the wills are earlier in date than the Pinners' Book, they have been included to provide as

53. For example: 'Item paid to [Thomas] Boyle, waxchandler, at various times, as appears by bill for the whole time 45s. 6d.', (**11**).

complete a documentation of the London pinners as possible. The later wills of the London wiresellers, who incoporated the pinners, have also been included for the same reason.

The pinners' wills were proved in three courts: the London court of Husting, and in the two ecclesiastical courts of the Archdeacon and the Commissary. The wills are printed here in chronological sequence, regardless of the place of probate.

THE PINNERS' AND WIRESELLERS' BOOK 1462–1511

[Calendar]
ff.1–6v. The calendar is written on six leaves and inserted as a separate leaflet into the front of the volume. It is written in black and red, and notes the feast days of the specifically London saints such as the translation of Erkenwald, bishop of London (14 November), who died in 693.

[The Pinners' Ordinances 1356][54]

1. [f. 7] To the Mayor and Aldermen of the City of London. The poor men of the City called Pinners ask that since their craft is much slandered for false work wrought by members of the craft that they may be ruled in the same way as other crafts in the City. And that the points and ordinances underwritten may be granted for the salvation of the craft and the profit of the people. And that six or four of the best [men] of the same craft be chosen and sworn to keep and maintain the ordinances afore-named if they be acceptable and appropriate.

[1.] First, that no foreign should hold house or shop in the City or the suburbs thereof nor sell nor buy anything concerned with the craft before he be made a free man of the City after he has been examined by the masters to see that he be able and skilled in the craft.

[2.] Also if any foreign come into the aforesaid City to work and make profit by the same craft he shall do nothing at it before he has presented himself to the masters of the craft and they have examined him as to his deeds and doings. And upon that shall be decided what he may reasonably take weekly for his labour so that the master may maintain his profit and the servant make an honest living.

54. The original ordinances copied into the City of London's Letter Book G were written in Anglo-Norman, see *LBG*, pp. 63–4. The Cardmakers (makers of implements used for carding wool) presented almost identical articles to those of the Pinners at the same time. In the Pinners' and Wiresellers' Book the fourteenth-century ordinances have been translated by the fifteenth century scribe into English.

[3.] Also no man of the craft shall procure, nor cause to be procured, either secretly or openly, another man's servant or *allowe*[55] whereby the master is worse served, whether by day or night, on pain of paying 40 shillings to the Chamber of the Guildhall as soon as he is convicted.

[f. 7v.] [4.] And if any such servant be alienated (*aloigned*) from his master in such a way then the master may, without any offence to any man, take back his aforesaid servant or *allowe*.

[5.] Also if any servant of the craft who has well and truly served his master should fall ill, so that he cannot keep himself, that he should be looked after and supported by the good folk of the craft until such time as he may himself find help and maintenance.

[6.] Also if any servant of the craft be of evil disposition, accustomed to do evil and will not be corrected by the good men of the craft, once he is found guilty of falseness to the value of 12d., he shall foreswear the craft until he may have better grace.

[7.] Also that no man of the craft shall take an apprentice or *allowe* unless he is himself a freeman of the same City. And that no man take any *allowe* unless he be approved by the masters of the craft to be skilled in that craft. And if there is any *allowe* who is not so capable then he shall leave the craft altogether unless he will become an apprentice.

[8.] Also if any of the craft be found working in the City in secret or openly, or selling (*chaffryng*) the products of the craft against the form above written, on discovery, the work or merchandise shall be forfeit to the use of the Chamber [of the Guildhall].

[9.] Also if any false or poor work be found in the City after the deliberation of the mayor, aldermen and masters of the craft, that work shall be seized and taken [f. 8] before the aforesaid mayor and aldermen to be adjudged whether it is good or bad.

[10.] Also that no man of the same craft shall take an apprentice unless he is witnessed by the good men of the same craft sworn as beforesaid, to be a man suitable (*convenable*), sufficient and cunning to keep, inform and teach his apprentice, for a term of seven years, as is the custom in the city, and no lesser term, on pain of losing his franchise.

[11.] Also that no man of the same craft may set to work any woman except his own wedded wife or daughter, and that no one of the craft shall be so hardy as to work by night nor on a Saturday on the eve of a double feast, once noon has been rung in the parish where he lives.

55. A hired worker, see Lisa Jefferson ed., *Wardens' Accounts and Court Minute Books of the Goldsmiths' Mystery of London, 1334–1446* (Woodbridge, 2003), pp. xxxiv-xxxv.

[12.] Also that no man of the craft shall open his shop on Sunday. Should any stranger wish to buy any merchandise on the Sunday then they should lead him to their houses in order to make it easier for travellers.

[13.] Also if any man of the craft be found by its sworn men acting against the ordinances, or any points thereof, he shall on the first occasion pay 40d. And at the second offence 3s. 4d. And at the third offence 10s. And at the fourth offence 20s. And all the work that may be found by the sworn men to be made contrary to these ordinances, to be forfeited to the Chamber [of the Guildhall].

[14.] Also that no man of the craft is to be so hardy as to [f. 8v.] defy or reprove the sworn men of the craft when they come to his house on their lawful business.

These articles are entered in the book with the letter G folio 48.[56]

[f. 9] Let it be remembered that Geoffrey Wade, Umper, John Vicary and Edmund Legge, Wardens of the craft of Pinners in the City of London have laboured well and truly to get the Exemplification under the king's great seal and therefore paid only for the weal of the craft, whereof [this is a] copy. And the same Exemplification under the king's great seal is in the keeping of the wardens of the Cutlers and at all times it shall be ready to be shown and delivered to you.[57]

2. [f. 9v.] [**The Pinners' 'Charter' 1463**][58]

Edward, by the grace of God king of England and France and lord of Ireland to the sheriffs of London and Middlesex... And also furthermore that where the artificers handcraftsmen and women resident and inhabiting and dwelling in the King's most noble and famous city of London and in other cities, towns, boroughs and villages within his noble realm of England and lordship of Wales have piteously shown and complained in the said parliament that they all, in general and everyone of them, be greatly impoverished, grievously hurt and hindered of their daily increase and daily living by the great multitude of divers goods and wares pertaining to their crafts and occupations being full wrought and ready made for sale, as both by the hands of strangers being the king's enemies as others brought in to the said realm and Wales from beyond the sea and by merchant strangers as well as denizens and other persons whereof the most part in substance is deceptive and not wrought in regard for any man's occupation or profit; wherefore the said artificers may not live by

56. London Metropolitan Archives, Corporation of London Letter Book G, f. 48
57. See **4**. This is the only instance in the book when the wardens presenting the accounts address the other pinners directly.
58. 3 Edward IV c.4, *SR*, vol. ii, pp. 396–98; see Rosemary Horrox, ed., *Parliament Rolls of Medieval England 1275–1504* (London, 2005) vol. xiii, pp. 113–115.

their crafts and occupations as they did in days passed, but many of them, householders as well as journeymen, servants and apprentices in great number are at this time unoccupied and live in great idleness, poverty and ruin.

Therefore the king our sovereign lord, in consideration of the above, to the pleasure of God and the eschewing of idleness, mother of all vices and mischiefs, and in amendment of the common weal of this his land hath, by the said advice and assent of his lords, spiritual and temporal, and commons in the said parliament assembled and by authority of the same ordained and [f. 10] established that no merchant, the king's born subject, denizen or stranger, nor any other person, after the next feast of St. Michael the Archangel, may bring, send or convey or cause to be brought, conveyed or sent, into this realm of England and lordship of Wales, that is any of the wares or things written below, that is to say: woollen bonnets, woollen cloth, laces, *corses* [bands?], ribbons, fringes of silk and of thread, threaded laces, thrown silk or silk in any wise embroidered, golden laces, *tires* [trimmings?] of silk or of gold, saddles, stirrups or any harness belonging to saddlers, spurs, bosses of bridles (*moleyns*), andirons, gridirons, any manner of locks, hammers, pincers, firetongs, dripping pans, dice, tennis balls, points, laces, purses, gloves, girdles, harness for girdles of iron, or latten or steel or tin or alloy (*alkomay*); nor anything wrought of any tawed leather, any manner of leatherware, tawed boots, shoes, galoshes or *cockes* (cork-soled sandals?), knives, daggers or woodknives, bodkins, shears for tailors, scissors, razors, sheaths, cards for playing, pins, pattens, packneedles; any manner of painted ware, forcers, caskets, rings of copper gilt, or latten, chafing dishes, candlesticks hanging or standing, washing bowls, chafing bowls,[59] sacring bells, rings for curtains, ladles, skimmers, counterfeit basins, ewers, hats, brushes, cards for wool or white wire, or anything to be offered or sold within this realm or Wales by way of merchandise upon pain of forfeiting everyone of them, at any time: and as often as they are found in the hands of any person or persons, to be sold: the one half thereof to our sovereign lord the king and the other half to him that seizeth it first for the king: the seizer's half to be delivered to him [through] the escheator of the shire or of the place where the seizer shall be, and by indenture between them to be made and the escheator to answer for the same in his account [f. 10v.].

Provided also that all wares and goods made and wrought in Ireland or Wales may be brought and sold in this realm of England, as they were wont before the making of this ordinance.

Provided always that if any of the aforesaid wares or goods made out of this land be taken over the sea without fraud or collusion or come into this realm or Wales by way of wreck, that they in no wise be included within

59. A vessel to hold burning charcoal, i.e. a portable grate or brazier.

this ordinance but that they may be sold within this realm or Wales, this ordinance notwithstanding.

And he also has ordained by the said authority that the masters or wardens for the time being of every craft and mystery in every city, borough, town and village where any such craft and mystery is used to have sufficient power and authority in every city, borough, town or village whereat they before the time being were master or wardens of any such craft or mystery; and the mayor of such city, town, borough or village for the time being, if there be any mayor thereof, or the bailiff or bailiffs of such city, borough or village for the time being, if any bailiffs or bailiff thereof be, and no mayor or sergeant or other officer to them assigned by the said mayor, bailiff or bailiffs; and in every city, borough, town or village where any such craft or mystery is used wherein be no masters or wardens of any such craft or mystery, that the masters or wardens of crafts or mysteries of the city, borough, town or village thereto next adjoining, and the constable of such city, town, borough or village have power and authority to search in their own crafts and mysteries offering for sale any of the said goods as well within the cities, boroughs, towns or villages of this realm and Wales and within the liberties and franchises of the same cities, towns, boroughs and villages, at all reasonable times, [f.11] by day or night, in fairs, markets, open shops and warehouses and all manner such chaffer, wares and merchandise to each of their crafts and mysteries appertaining;
as shall be made by any manner of alien craftsmen or women or any other person within this realm or Wales or shall, at any time, be occupied by any of the same crafts or mysteries in whose hands they may be found.

Provided always that the said masters or wardens and others named in this ordinance as searchers do not enter into any place exempt by privilege, franchise, grant or custom to make pins, any search as it is aforesaid [except by the oversight of] the officer of every such exempt place where any such search shall happen to be made.

And if the said searchers find by the same search that such chaffers, wares or merchandise, or any part thereof, be not clean, true and [sale]able chaffer, wares or merchandise, and truly made and wrought as it ought to be, and that duly proved, that then it will be lawful for such searchers to take and seize as things forfeited all such chaffer, wares or merchandise that so shall be found not good, clean, true and [sale]able, not truly wrought, the one half thereof to belong to the king our said sovereign lord and the other half to such masters or wardens that have searched and found it.

And that this ordinance shall stand and be in force as long as it shall please the king our said sovereign lord.

[Latin] Let it be publicly proclaimed for our part where it is most expedient within your bailiwick, both within the liberty and outside, from time to time as often as is necessary, and let it be held and observed in all and singular its articles according to the form noted above. Westminster 28 July 3 Edward IV [1463].

[In a later hand] This charter was granted to the pinmakers of London the 28 July in the third year of King Edward the fourth 1464 [recte 1463].

3. [f. 12] The account of Geoffrey Wade, umper, John Vicary and Edmund Legge, wardens of the craft of Pinners of the city of London who truly and diligently have made these accounts before the said craft in the Girdlers' Hall,[60] from 12 November, the 2nd year of our liege lord King Edward IV [1462] to 15 November the 4th year of the same King Edward IV [1464] for 2 complete years.

Receipts
First received for the coming of Thomas Tarte and his wife to be made brother and sister of the fraternity of the Pinners' craft 5s.
Item for Joan the wife of John Ronell to make her a sister 20d.
Item likewise for Isabel the wife of Robert Rumbold to make her a sister of the same craft 20d.
Item Robert Rumbold and John Sterne have given to the craft [the proceeds] of a wager between them 16d.
Item for a fine from Gervase Cotrell 6d.
Item of John Sterne and his wife to be made brother and sister 5s.
Item of William Michell for costs of his wife's burying 6s. 8d.
Item of John Pitte for his wife to be a sister 20d.
Item received of the craft in Lent for our place in Girdlers' Hall 7s. 9d.
Item for the wife of Thomas Manger for [past] quarterage[61] 3s. 4d.
[f. 12v.] Item for the incoming of Thomas Manger to be a brother 3s. 4d.
Item received of Richard Hughis for Gervase Cotrell as a gift to the said craft 8d.
Item of [John] Pitte's wife for coming in again 2s.
Item of Robert Hill for a fine for employing a servant of Richard Beaumont 20d.
Item received for quarterage during the said 2 years £3 2s. 6d.
Item received of Robert Rumbold and John Bartlet for a gift of the young men of the craft as appears by their bill 21d.
Total £5 6s. 6d.

4. [f. 13] Costs and expenses are as follows:
These are the parcels of the costs and expenses that the umper and wardens of the said craft [incurred] during their time
First paid for 13 skins of parchment for this new book 2s. 5d.
Item paid for a calendar for the same book 10d.
Item paid for binding, making and clasps of the same book 12d.

60. The Girdlers' Hall was off Bassishaw Street
61. Quarterage: the members' regular payment or subscription.

Item to making of 2 bills of divers articles for the said craft 5d.
Item paid to a yeoman of the Chamber for taking a distress [*i.e.* distraint] of one Agnes Smyth a foreign[62] 6d.
Item for a little new chest for our craft 2s.
Item paid to Richard Quycke our beadle 1 April 4 Edward IV [1464] towards his wages 3s.
Item paid the same day to Barette Cutler[63] and his fellowship for the weal of our craft and the suit at Westminster 6s. 8d.
Item to Richard Quycke on St Katherine's day [25 November] 3 Edward IV [1463] towards his wages 3s. 8d.
Item 7 May in the same year for hire of a barge for our fellowship 6d.
Item paid for a breakfast for our fellowship the same time 3d.
Item with expenses with William Overy at the same time 3d.
Item on 15 May for costs of the same William Overy [64] 2d.
[In a later hand] 3 Edward IV in May [1463] paid for the hire of a barge for our craft 6d.; paid for a breakfast 7d.
[f. 13v.] Item paid on 11 May for barge hire 6d.
Item paid for a writ for William Taylour and his fellowship who are foreigns 4s. 7d.
Item for making 2 obligations[65] for William Taylour and a Fleming 6d.
Item for barge hire on 13 May 6d.
Item to the beadle of the Pointmakers' craft 2d.
Item to the sexton of Elsyng Spital[66] for the first year 8d.
Item for the scouring of the candlestick at Elsyng Spital 2d.
Item in expenses for William Overy two more times 14d.
Item paid at the same time for boat hire twice for William Overy 5d.
Item to the waxchandler's man for setting up our lights at St James[67] and at Elsyng Spital 3d.
Item for making of our table for the fraternity of St James 8d.
Item for a trental for the fraternity of our craft for the first year 2s. 6d.
Item for a trental for Thomas Manger's wife 2s. 6d.
Item for a trental for the wife of Geoffrey Prany 2s. 6d.
Item for boat hire going with the sheriff toWestminster 13d.
Item for boat hire going with the mayor to Westminster 13d.
Item paid to our brethren that did not dine at the mayor's dinner, to their breakfast at the same time 16d.
[f. 14]

62. Foreign/forin: someone who was not free of the City, i.e. not a citizen.
63. Probably Thomas Barette, cutler, who died in 1466.
64. William Overy was a stockfishmonger and Merchant Adventurer. For his career, see Anne F. Sutton, 'Caxton was a Mercer: his Social Milieu and Friends' in Nicholas Rogers ed., *England in the Fifteenth Century: Proceedings of the 1992 Harlaxton Symposium* (Stamford, 1994), pp. 118–148, esp. pp. 127–132.
65. An obligation: a legal term for a bond or covenant
66. Elsyng Spital was founded in 1331 by the will of William Elsyng as a hospital for blind priests, but became a priory hospital for canons regular by 1353, see Barron and Davies, *Religious Houses*, pp. 165–168.
67. Probably the Hospital of St James, Westminster, see *ibid.* pp. 177–181.

Item paid in alms to bury Gamlyn's wife 12d.
Item to the yeoman of the Chamber to fetch Richard Sponelay, foreign, to the Chamberlain 4d.
Item to Barette Cutler and his fellowship 3 December 3 Edward IV [1463], for the weal of our craft and the suit at Westminster 24s. 8d.
Item paid to the Clerk of the Parliament 12d.
Item paid to a sergeant of the mayor's for his labour and his dinner for [going] with us to a common search with Girdlers and Pointmakers 2s.
Item to [Thomas] Barette, when he came from Northampton 3s. 4d.
Item for costs of sending to the king at Northampton 20d.
Item in costs at Salisbury for the searching for and burning of pins 2s. 4d.
Item for expenses with William Overy at a dinner 12d.
Item delivered to Thomas Barette for the suit of the proclamation 20d.
Item delivered to Thomas Barette at another time for William Overy 8s.
Item delivered to the escheator at the Exchequer 14d.
Item for costs of burning of certain pins and other ware at the standard at Cheap 12d.
Item for 2 trentals, one for the wife of [William] Michell and another for the wife of [John] Pitte 5s.
Item to William Michell for pins for the sisters at St James[68] 8d.
[f. 14v.] Item to the sexton of Elsyng Spital 8d.
Item for a trental for all the fraternity 2s. 6d.
Item for 5 dozen trenchers 15d.
Item for a kitchen cloth 8d.
Item for boat hire the second year with the sheriffs to Westminster 12d.
Item paid for the Exemplification for our craft which lies with the craft of Cutlers 10s.
Item for costs at Stourbridge (*Sturbrigge*)[69] for searching and burning certain ware and pins 2s. 6d.
Item for Richard Quycke's wages for the second year 6s. 8d.
Item for a hood for the same Richard Quycke 5s.
Item for the master of St James, master Malmesbury, for a hood of a yard and three-quarter price[70] 6s. 2d.
Item to the waxchandlers as per bill 52s. 4d.
Item to John Smale for costs as per bill 6s. 8d.
Item for hire of Girdlers' Hall for 2 years 4s.
Item for scouring the vessels and washing the cloths there 12d.
Sum of payments £10 5s. 4d.

68. Four alms-sisters lived in the Hospital of St James, see G. Rosser, *Medieval Westminster* (Oxford, 1989), pp. 307–310.
69. Stourbridge Fair: one of the great regional fairs of the period, held in Cambridge.
70. Roger Malmesbury occurs as Master of the Hospital of St James, 1463–7, Barron and Davies, *Religious Houses,* p. 181.

5. [f. 15] Be it remembered that Geoffrey Wade, umper, John Vicary and Edmund Legge, wardens of the craft of Pinners of the city of London on 15 November 4 Edward IV [1464] reckoned and accounted for all things before the brethren of the said craft in the tavern at the sign of the Mermaid in Bread Street. After their dinner held there, the aforesaid umper and wardens, by the assent of all the brethren, delivered into the hands of William Machon, umper, Henry Somer and Robert Rumbold, wardens of the same craft, newly chosen for the next 2 years after the aforesaid date, the sum of £18 0s. 6d.
Item delivered into the hands of the new umper and wardens, pertaining to the said sum, a ring of gold laid in the box as a pledge by William Clerk 5s. 10d.

6. [f. 15v.] The account of William Machon, umper, Henry Somer and Robert Rumbold, wardens of the craft [who] rendered their account before the craft in the Girdlers' Hall of London from 15 November 4 Edward IV [1464] to 3 November 6 Edward IV [1466].
Receipts
First received of John Couper for not coming to the Girdlers' Hall when summoned 4d.
Item of Thomas Tarte at the same time for the the same cause 4d.
Item of Thomas Newlyn for like cause 4d.
Item of Richard Hughis for like cause 6d.
Item of Richard Beaumont for like cause 6d.
Item of John Plays for like cause 2d.
Item received of William Vyan for setting a child to work before he was bound apprentice, for setting to work a servant of Richard Hughis and for working after 7 o'clock in winter nights 4s. whereof the Chamber has had 2s. and so to us 2s.
Item received of Robert Hill 20d., in part payment of 3s. 4d. for taking an apprentice illicitly *(under colour*) and giving him wages, and for making unclean wares 20d. sum 3s. 4d.
Item received of Richard Burgeys for taking in John Herte to work in our fellowship part payment of 5s. 4s.
[f. 16] Item received of Richard Sponeley, in part [payment of] 5s. for his entry 20d.
Item of John Jenkyn for working out of the franchise, in part payment of 20d. 12d.
Item of Richard Beaumont for working on Saturday after 12 o'clock 10d.
Item received of John Symmes for making unclean ware 12d.
Item received of William Parker by the hand of Edmund Legge for taking on the same [William] Parker to work in the fellowship 3s. 4d.
Item of Thomas Wakelyn for working late after 7 o'clock in winter 12d.
Item received of Richard Beaumont for disobeying the wardens contrary to good reason and rules 3s.
Item of Thomas Lovesome for his incoming 4s.

Item of William Savage for working at St Katherine's 3s. 4d.
Item of John Shore for deceiving and defying the wardens 3s. 4d.
Item received of William Michell for entering his wife Agnes to be a sister 20d.
Item likewise of Geoffrey Prany for entering Joan, his wife 20d.
Item of John Gerveys for defying (*missaid*) the Wardens 8d.
Item the said umper and wardens have received in quarterage from the brothers and sisters during their time £3 16s. 0d.
Item received of Geoffrey Prany for John Smyth to become a workman in the craft 3s. 4d.
Sum of all receipts £5 17s. 4d.

7. [f. 16v.] Item received of William Parker of London, pinner, in part payment of 40s. which he is bound to pay at 8d. on Saturday every week, by an obligation of 100s. to William Machon, Henry Somer and Robert Rumbold to the intent that, when the said sum is paid off, the umper and wardens at that time shall, upon due and reasonable warning, present the said [William] Parker to the Chamberlain of London and do necessary [things] for the same [William] Parker, at his cost, to be admitted and made freeman of the said craft without paying any other fine. 32s. 8d.
Item likewise received of Thomas Lovesome of London, pinner, in part payment of 40s. for which he is bound under obligation to the said William Machon, Henry Somer and Robert Rumbold to pay 8d. a week each Saturday with the intention of making him a freeman in the same way as the said [William] Parker 19s. 4d.
Sum of these receipts £2 12s. 0d.
Sum total of all receipts £8 9s. 4d.

8. [f. 17] The parcels of costs and expenses incurred by the umper and wardens during their time:
First paid for woollen cloth for the craft for the queen's coronation [1465][71] 15s.
Item for a trental of masses for Geoffrey Wade's wife 2s. 6d.
Item for a trental of masses for the brothers and sisters 2s. 6d.
Item for setting up the light before St James 2d.
Item for expenses at the same time 3d.
Item for lighting the light at Elsyng Spital at that time 16d.
Item expenses on the day of the search 9d.
Item to the sisters of St James 600 pins price 11d.
Item for boat hire with the sheriffs to Westminster, the first year 9d. and the second year 11d. total 20d.
Item for boat hire with the mayor 8d.
Item for 1500 pins given to the wife of William Overy 18d.
Item paid to the beadle for his wages for 2 years 13s. 4d.

71. Elizabeth Woodville, queen of Edward IV. They were married in secret in May 1464, in defiance of Richard Neville, earl of Warwick, who had planned a marriage for the king, to a foreign princess. Elizabeth came to London for her coronation in May 1465.

Item given to 6 people at the time of the mayor's dinner 12d.
Item spent the day of our search 3s. 0½d.
Item for an obligation with condition 4d.
[f. 17v.] Item for searching at the Waterside 12d.
Item for searching at Stourbridge 16d.
Item to both Edmund Legge and Robert Rumbold 20d. each to ride with the queen at her coronation 3s. 4d.
Item for a trental of masses at Whitefriars for Katherine Pitte 2s. 6d.
Item for an obligation with condition 4d.
Item for bearing the light to St James 2d.
Item for a trental of masses at Whitefriars for the brothers and sisters 2s. 6d.
Item for a trental of masses for Geoffrey Wade 2s. 6d.
Item for the Girdlers' Hall for 2 years 4s.
Item for washing and keeping of the cloths and vessels 12d.
Item to [Thomas] Boyle, waxchandler, throughout the time, as appears by divers bills 20s. 9d.
Item for making and writing this account 16d.
Item paid for a trental of masses at Whitefriars for Geoffrey Prany 2s. 6d.
Item for a trental of masses there for John Legge 2s. 6d.
Item for boat hire with the mayor in both years 11½d.
Item for entering 2 sisters into the table of our brotherhood and removing [those] of them passed to God and set among the dead 2d.
Item paid to Richard Quycke our beadle for his half hood 2s. 6d.
Sum total of all costs and payments £4 11s. 7d.

9.[f. 18] Total clear of increases in their time £3 17s. 9d.
The which sum of £3 17s. 9d. and £18 0s. 6d.was delivered to William Machon, umper, Henry Somer and Robert Rumbold, wardens, by Geoffrey Wade, John Vicary and Edmund Legge, their predecessors, their account being made in the Girdlers' Hall before all the brethren 3 November 6 Edward IV [1466] to John Couper, umper, Edmund Legge and Thomas Tarte, wardens, now chosen for the next 2 years.
Sum total clear to the craft £21 18s. 3d.

10. [f. 18v.] The account of John Couper, umper, Edmund Legge and Thomas Tarte, wardens of the craft in the Girdlers' Hall of London, 19 December 8 Edward IV [1468].
Receipts
First received of [?John] Cadman's son 12d.
Item of [Thomas] Newlyn for a fine 8d.
Item received of [William] Vyan 12d.
Item received of Robert Hill 20d.
Item received of [John] Bartlet's wife to be a sister 20d.
Item received of William Savage by a tally (*tayle*) 16d.
Item received for pins 5s. 4d.
Item received of John Bartlet for a fine 4d.

Item received of William Parker as it appears in the book of account 7s. 4d.
Item received of Thomas Lovesome 20s. 8d.
Item received for old nobles that were in our box 2s. 6d.
Sum of the receipts 42s. 3d.
[f. 19] Thomas Tampe owes the craft 13s. 4d. which Thomas Tarte has borrowed therefore to pay at the day of our account 13s. 4d.
The sum of the quarterage £3 2s. 4d.
Sum total of the receipts and quarterage £5 17s. 11d.

11. Costs [incurred by] the umpers and wardens in their term
First paid to the beadle for his wages 13s. 4d.
Item for a hood cloth to the beadle 5s. 2d.
Item for a hood cloth to the Master of St James, a yard and a quarter, price 6s. 10d.
Item for a trental for Joan Legge 2s. 6d.
Item for a trental for the wife of John Ronell 2s. 6d.
Item for a trental for John Legge 2s. 6d.
Item for a trental for the brothers and sisters 2s. 6d.
Item for taking a copy of the ordinances of the craft out of the mayor's court 3s.
Item for the scouring of the vessels and for the washing of the cloths of the craft for 2 years 2s.
Item delivered to the beadle for 200 pins of Flanders ware for a press for [William] Vyan 3d.[72]
[f. 19v.] Item paid to the sexton of Elsyng Spital and to the clerk of the said place 20d.
Item for boat hire with the sheriffs to Westminster 12d.
Item for boat hire with the mayor to Westminster 12d.
Item paid to [Thomas] Boyle, waxchandler, at various times, as appears by bill for the whole time 45s. 6d.
Item paid to the beadle and the waxchandler's men for setting up the light at St James 3d.
Item for boat hire with the sheriffs to Westminster 12d.
Item for a covered boat with the mayor to Westminster 2s. 10d.
Item for a trental for Richard Hughis 2s. 6d.
Item for a trental of masses at Whitefriars for the brethren and sisters 2s. 6d.
Item for a covered boat 2s. 10d.
Item for a trental of masses for Richard Andrew 2s. 6d.
Item for a yeoman of the Chamber 3 times 18d.
Item to the fellowship when the mayor went to Westminster 20d.
Item for an obligation for William Savage 2d.
Item for pins for the sisters 6d.
Item paid to the sexton of Elsyng Spital 12d.

72. It is not clear what this refers to.

Item for 2 torch bearers for Richard Andrew 8d.
Item for Girdlers' Hall for 2 years 4s.
Item for the scrivener's wages 16d.
Item for John Vicary for a sergeant to make him take his charge 20d.
Sum total of costs £5 16s. 8d.
[f. 20.] Sum total clear to the craft £22 0s. 9d.

12. [f. 20v.] The account of William Michell, umper, John Vicary and John Bartlet, wardens of the craft, made before the craft in the Girdlers' Hall of London, from 19 December 8 Edward IV [1468] to 24 November 49th year from the beginning of the reign of King Henry VI and from the taking again of his royal power, the first year [1470].

Receipts

First received of John Ronell for his wife to be a sister 20d.
Item received of John Roch for his admission to work 3s. 4d.
Item received of William Vyan as fine for setting a foreign on to work 3s. 4d..
Item received of Robert Rumbold for the burying of Thomas Cavell 2s.
Item received of William Hill a forfeit of pins for default of tally 14d.
Item received of Robert Hill for his entry as a brother 3s. 4d.
Item received of Richard Burgeys for an old debt 12d.
Item received of quarterage for the space of 2 years £3 0s. 6d.
Item received of Edward Lymsey for a licence to work in the craft 3s. 4d.
Sum total of all receipts £3 19s. 8d.

13. [f. 21] The parcel of costs and expenses of the umper and wardens during their term

First for a trental for Alice Vicary 2s. 6d.
Item for a trental for Margaret Ronell 2s. 6d.
Item paid to the sexton of Elsyng Spital for the space of 2 years 2s.
Item paid to the Whitefriars for the trental for the brothers and sisters for 2 years 5s.
Item delivered to the sisters of St James 1000 pins 16d.
Item paid to William Clerk for his wages for 2 years 13s. 4d.
Item for a trental for Amy Dadyngton 2s. 6d.
Item for boat hire for 2 years 10s. 8d.
Item for a trental for Margaret Cadman 2s. 6d.
Item for the Masons' Hall [73] 2s. 6d.
Item for drinking at St Katherine's when the king came up by water 3½d.
Item for boat hire to Westminster when the wardens were sent for by the king 4d.
Item paid for a trental for William Hill 2s. 6d.

73. The Masons' Hall was off Coleman Street.

Item paid for 5 yards of brown blue for the return of King Edward [IV] out the North 15s.
Item because William Hill did not have the full light Katherine his wife is rewarded 2s.
Item paid to [Thomas] Boyle, waxchandler, for wax as appears by a bill in various parcels 42s. 3d.
Item for the beadle's hood 5s.
Item for the writing of this account 12d.
Item for keeping the chest, washing the napery and cleaning the vessels 2s.
[f. 21v.] Item paid for the Girdlers' Hall for 2 years 4s.
Sum of all costs and payments £5 16s. 10½d

Be it remembered that William Michell, umper, John Vicary and John Bartlet, wardens of the craft, on 26 November the 49th year from the beginning of the reign of King Henry VI and from the taking again of his royal power, the first year [1470] made their account before all the brethren after dinner in the brewhouse at the sign of the Rose in the Old Jewry and delivered, on behalf of the craft into the hands of Henry Somer, umper, Robert Rumbold and John Plays, wardens, now chosen for the next 2 years £20 3s. 6½d.

14. [f. 22v.] The account of Henry Somer, umper, Robert Rumbold and John Plays, wardens of the craft, made before the craft in the Armourers' Hall[74] of London from 26 November the 49th year from the beginning of the reign of King Henry VI and from the taking again of his royal power, the first year [1470] to 17 November 12 Edward IV [1472].
Receipts
First received of John Wekys for entry as a brother of the craft 13s. 4d.
Item received of John Stoneham for keeping open shop before he was made a freeman 2s. 1d.
Item received of William Castell in part payment of a larger sum for his being received as a workman into the craft 16d.
Item received of Thomas Tarte for not coming to the Girdlers' Hall when summoned 4d.
Item received of Richard Beaumont for like cause 6d.
Item received of John Newlyn for disobeying the wardens 3s. 4d.
Item received of William Parker for entry into the craft as a brother 3s. 4d.
Item received of William Haket to be received as a workman into the craft 3s. 4d.
[f. 23] Item received of John Synet for a trespass against the rules of the craft
3s. 4d.

74. The Armourers' Hall stood at the corner of Coleman Street and London Wall.

Item received of [?Thomas] Arnold for selling Flemish pins as English ones 20d.
Item received of John Kyrkeby in part payment of a larger sum 6d.
Item received from the brothers and sisters in quarterage for 2 years £3 3s. 10d.
Sum of receipts £4 16s. 11d.

15. The parcels of costs and expenses incurred by the umper and wardens during their term of office.
First paid at the Armourers' Hall on St Paul's day[75] as a reward to the beadle 2d.
Item paid to the mayor's clerk for making a bill 1d.
Item paid to an officer of the Chamber to fetch Thomas Sutton, [William] Michell's apprentice 4d.
Item paid to Richard Quycke as his salary was behindhand 3s. 4d.
Item paid to the sexton at Elsyng Spital 8d.
Item paid to the waxchandlers' man for setting the wax at St James 2d.
Item paid to the Whitefriars for the dirge on St James's day [25 July] 2s. 6d.
[f. 23v.] Item paid for a trental of masses for John Sterne 2s. 6d.
Item paid for a trental of masses for Margaret Boges 2s. 6d.
Item paid to the wardens of the Armourers for quarter day 20d.
Item paid for boat hire for the sheriffs 12d.
Item paid for boat hire for the mayor 2s. 8d.
Item paid for rushes 2d.
Item paid for a trental of masses for John Cadman 2s. 6d.
Item paid for an obligation on John Kirkeby 4d.
Item paid for a trental of masses for Thomas Newlyn 2s. 6d.
Item paid to the sexton of Elsyng Spital 8d.
Item paid for the setting up of the light at St James 2d.
Item paid for a breakfast and boat hire at the same time 3d.
Item paid for entering the names of the brothers and sisters in the table 2d.
Item paid for a trental for all the brothers and sisters 2s. 6d.
Item paid for a trental for John Ronell 2s. 6d.
Item paid for boat hire with the sheriffs 12d.
Item paid for boat hire with the mayor 12d.
Item paid to the wardens of the Armourers for hire of their hall 3s. 4d.
Item paid to Robert Rumbold for keeping and washing the cloths 16d.
Item paid to William Clerk for his salary 13s. 4d.
Item paid to William Clerk for his hood cloth 4s. 10d.
Item paid to the waxchandler, as appears by his bill 49s. 6d.
Item paid to John Plays for 900 pins 12d.
Item paid for writing the account 12d.
Sum of all payments £5 5s. 8d.

75. Probably the Conversion of St Paul, 25 January.

[f. 24] Be it remembered that Henry Somer, Robert Rumbold and John Plays, wardens of the craft on 19 November 1472, accounted to the craft after dinner in the Armourers' Hall. The aforesaid umper and wardens have, on behalf of the said craft, delivered into the hands of William Machon, umper, Edmund Legge and John Bartlet, the newly chosen wardens for the next 2 years £19 14s. 9½d.

16. [f. 24v.] The account of William Machon, Robert Rumbold and John Bartlet, wardens of the craft, who gave their account before the said craft in the Armourers' Hall of London on 14 November 15 Edward IV [1475].
Receipts
First received of John Newlyn to be a brother 3s. 4d.
Item received of William Vyan to be a brother 3s.b4d.
Item received of John Wekys for late working 20d.
Item received of John Proude for coming late to [Edmund] Legge's mass 2d.
Item received of William Mynte to be a brother 6s. 8d.
Item received of all the brethren and the fellowship as appears by a bill 28s.
Item received in quarterage for 3 years £4 0s. 8d.
Item received by Thomas Tarte 2s.
Sum of receipts £6 13s. 2d.

17. [f. 25] The parcels of costs and expenses of the said umper and wardens during their time in office:
First paid for the Armourers' Hall for three years 10s.
Item paid to the [White]friars for a trental for [John] Sterne 2s. 6d.
Item paid for a trental for Edmund Legge 2s. 6d.
Item paid for a trental for William Michell 2s. 6d.
Item paid for a trental for [John] Wekys's wife 2s. 6d.
Item paid to the friars for 3 trentals for 3 years 7s. 6d.
Item paid to the sexton of Elsyng Spital 8d.
Item paid for setting up the light of St James 4d.
Item paid for 800 pins for the sisters 12d.
Item paid for 3 years going to Westminster with the mayor and sheriffs 6s. 3d.
Item paid for setting up the light of St James at [White]friars for 2 years 6d.
Item paid to the [White]friars for singing the mass for 2 years 3s. 4d.
Item paid to John Plays when the king came out of the north 3s. 4d
Item paid to Richard Quycke for his hood 4s. 4d.
Item paid to the said Richard for his wages for 3 years 20s.
[f. 25v.] Item paid for keeping the vessels and cloths of the craft for 3 years 3s.
Item paid for divers costs of St James £3 5s. 8d.
Item paid for the waxchandler for 3 years 38s.
Item paid for mending the table of the brothers and sisters 4d.
Item for the making of this account 8d.

Item paid for 2 gown cloths of murrey[76] 13s. 4d.
Sum of payments [crossed out £8 15s. 7d.] £9 8s. 9d.

18. [f. 26] Be it remembered that John Vicary, umper, Thomas Tarte and Robert Hill, wardens of the craft, chosen on 16 November 15 Edward IV [1475], the accounts having been given after the dinner, before the brethren in the Armourers' Hall in Coleman Street, received on behalf of the craft from William Machon, late umper, Robert Rumbold and John Bartlet, late wardens of the craft £14 in ready money.
Item an obligation of £3 in which the late Edmund Legge stood bound.

19. [f. 26v.] The account of John Vicary, umper, John Plays and Robert Hill, wardens of the craft of pinners of the City of London which they gave, truly and diligently to the craft in the Armourers' Hall of London, [for the period] from 15 November 17 (*recte* 15) Edward IV [1475] to the 22 November [1477].
Receipts
First from quarterage of the bretheren and sisters for 2 years 51s.
Item received of Robert Hill for his wife to be a sister 20d.
Item received from the sale of Thomas Tarte's goods in money 18s. 3d.
Item received of Robert Hill for Joan his wife to be a sister 20d.
Item received of Richard Quycke for his wife's light 2s. 6d.
Item received of [?John] Newlyn for failure to appear 4d.
Item received of William Parker for failure to appear 4d.
Sum £3 15s. 9d.

20. [f. 27.] The parcels of the costs and expenses had by the said umper and wardens during their term of office
Costs
First a trental for Robert Rumbold's wife 2s. 6d.
Item a trental paid for Thomas Tarte 2s. 6d.
Item a trental for [Robert] Hill's wife 2s. 6d.
Item 2 trentals at the [White]friars for 2 years 5s.
Item a reward for the [White]friars for singing for 2 years 3s. 4d.
Item for the beadle's wages for 2 years 13s. 4d.
Item the Armourers' Hall for 2 years 6s. 8d.
Item for arrears of our supper 5s. 2d.
Item the costs of the plea of Thomas Tarte 8s.
Item for charity 18d.
Item for setting up the light at the [White]friars before St James for 2 years 8d.
Item for Snow the sergeant for searching the foreigns 12d.
Item for keeping the vessels for 2 years 2s.
Item for searching at Guildhall for the wiredrawers 4d.

76. Murrey cloth: a dark red cloth named from *morum*, Latin for mulberry.

Item to [Gervase] Cotrell for bringing [Thomas] Arnolde and [Robert] Cadman to the Chamber 4d.
Item boat hire to Westminster for 2 years 4s.
Item to the waxchandler as appears by bill 30s.
Sum £4 9s. 5d.

21. [f. 27v.] Be it remembered that Robert Rumbold, umper, John Bartlet and William Parker, wardens of the craft, newly chosen on 25 November 17 Edward IV [1477], the accounts having been given after dinner in the Armourers' Hall, received from John Vicary, umper, John Plays and Robert Hill [their predecessors] on behalf of the said craft £10 6s. 4 d. in ready money.
Item there remains in the hands of Katherine Hill from the goods of Thomas Tarte as appears by bill 18s. 5d.
Item an obligation for £3 owed by Edmund Legge, deceased.
Item an obligation for £3 owed by Thomas Tarte, deceased, of which was paid 25s. 11d.

22. [f. 28] The account of Robert Rumbold, umper, John Bartlet and William Parker, wardens of the craft, made before the craft in Pinners' Hall[77] [for the period] 25 November 17 Edward IV [1477] to 26 November 21 Edward IV [1481]
Receipts
First received of Katherine Hill for [Thomas] Tarte's goods 15s. 3d.
Item received of John Newlyn for a supper 8d.
Item received of Robert Archer for failing to appear 2d.
Item received of Richard Coke for like cause 2d.
Item received of William Knotte for like offence 2d.
Item received of Richard Beaumont the younger for like cause 2d.
Item received of William Leche to be admitted to the craft as a brother 4s.
Item received of Robert Rumbold for 12,000 pins forfeited to the craft 8s.
Item received of John Stoneham for admission to the craft as a brother 3s. 4d.
[f. 28v.] Item received of Robert Cokkes, sergeant 6s. 8d.
Item received of Geoffrey Moreton, sergeant 6s. 8d.
Item received of Robert Danyell, sergeant 6s. 8d.
Item received of Thomas Alwyn, sergeant 3s. 4d.
Item received of William Parker for his wife to be admitted a sister 20d.
Item received of Robert Rumbold for his wife to be admitted a sister 20d.
Item received of Margaret Hall to be admitted as a freewoman of the craft 10s.

77. The Pinners' Hall was in Adel Street, off Wood Street, in Cripplegate Ward.

Item received for drinking 24s. 8½d.
Item received of John Bradley to be admitted into the craft as a freeman 13s. 4d.
Item received of Roger Florence for rent for the Christmas quarter 2s.
Item received of Robert Howton to be admitted a brother 3s. 4d.
Item received of William Tytlay 13s. 4d.
Item received of John Randolf for rent 2s. 4d.
Item received of Isabell Goor for Easter quarter 10d.
Item received of [Richard] Quycke for Michaelmas quarterage 20d.
Item received of Robert Ettell to become a brother 3s. 4d.
Item received for quarterage for 4 years £4 5s. 4d.
Item received of Edward Morys for a fine 16d.
Item received of Thomas Parys for his fine 6d.
[f. 29.] Item received of John Burford for a fine 14d.
Item received of Richard Burgeys for a fine 4d.
Item received of an obligation of Edmund Legge 30s.
Total receipts £12 12s. 1½d.

23. [f. 29v.] Payments
First paid for the carriage of [Thomas] Tarte's goods 8d.
Item paid as a reward to a yeoman of the Chamber for his office 4d.
Item paid to the man who worked for [Thomas] Tarte's goods 3s. 4d.
Item paid for a trental at the Whitefriars for Margaret Stodell 2s. 6d.
Item for making a bill 2d.
Item paid for Robert Cartleage[78] for a bill 12d.
Item paid for the same bill 3s. 4d.
Item paid for the summons of Thornell twice 8d.
Item paid for Thomas Hayns before the Chamberlain 4d.
Item paid for a new judas[79] 2s. 4d.
Item paid for a trental for all the brothers and sisters 2s. 6d.
Item paid for the mass on St James's day [25 July] 20d.
Item paid for boat hire to Westminster with the sheriffs 8d.
Item paid for [William] Parker at the mayor's commandment for imprisonment 16d.
Item paid to a yeoman of the Chamber for the search that was made for foreigns 8d.
[f. 30] Item paid for a trental for John Vicary 2s. 6d.
Item paid for a trental for the brothers and sisters 2s. 6d.
Item paid for the mass at the [White]friars 20d.
Item paid to the chandler 2d.
Item paid for the scouring of the candlesticks 3d.
Item paid to Richard Quycke for his wages 25s.
Item paid to the same Richard for a yard of cloth 3s. 6d.
Item paid for boat hire with the mayor 11d.

78. Robert Cartleage was a clerk of the mayor's court, see Barron, *London in the Later Middle Ages*, p. 194.
79. A judas was a seven-branch Paschal candlestick in churches.

Item paid for the Armourers' Hall for 2 years 6s. 8d.
Item paid to the chandler's man 2d.
Item paid for a trental of masses 2s. 6d.
Item paid to the singers of the mass 12d.
Item paid for the writing of names into the table 4d.
Item paid for John Plays to a yeoman of the Chamber 4d.
Item paid for boat hire with the sheriffs 11d.
Item paid for a trental for Robert Page 2s. 6d.
Item paid for an obligation with condition for Roger Florence 4d.
Item paid for boat hire with the mayor 9½d.
Item paid to a sergeant for Peter Colyns 12d.
Item paid to the chandler for lights 2d.
Item paid to the [White]friars at mass 12d.
Item paid for a trental of masses 2s. 6d.
[f. 30v.] Item paid for 2 dozen trenchers 2d.
Item paid for the plea of John Robson 8s. 2d.
Item paid for boat hire with the mayor and sheriffs 20d.
Item paid for keeping the vessels for 4 years 4s.
Item paid to the waxchandler, as appears by bill 46s. 7d.
Item paid for the indentures of the hall 2s. 4d.
Item paid for 15,000 of laths 5s.
Item paid for quarters and board 11s. 2d.
Item paid to the carpenter for his wages 15s.
Item paid for loam, sand and gravel 9s.
Item paid to the dauber and his man 25s.
Item paid for brick, lime and masons' work 11s. 8d.
Item paid for sprigg nails and ironwork 15s. 6d.
Item paid for carrying rubbish 3s. 4d.
Item paid for staining of the *halling*[80] 31s. 1d.
Item paid for *lyre*[81] and sewing of the same 22d.
Item paid for 12 pounds of red lead 18d.
Item paid for pigment (*moty*) 7½d.
Item paid for coal 7d.
Item paid for a table and 2 trestles 4s.
Item paid for 4 forms 16d.
Item paid to the raker and to the clerk 8d.
Item paid for mats in the hall and parlour 2s. 2d.
Item paid for rent for a whole year 20s.
Item paid for a lock 7d.
Item paid for divers repairs 3s. 2½d.
Item paid for a half year's rent of the hall 10s.
Item paid for writing this account 16d.
Sum total £10 16s. 9½d.

80. Word used to describe leather or cloth hangings in a hall.
81. A kind of binding or tape.

24. [f. 31]
Be it remembered that I John Plays, umper, William Parker and Robert Howton, wardens of the craft, now chosen and sworn on 27 November 21 Edward IV [1481], the accounts being made before the brothers after dinner in the Pinners' Hall, have received, on behalf of the craft, of Robert Rumbold, late umper, John Bartlet and William Parker, late wardens, in ready money £7 2s. 6d.
Item an obligation of Edmund Kyng of 40s. payable next Easter 10s.

25. [f. 31v.] The account of John Plays, umper, William Parker and Robert Howton, wardens of the craft, made before the brethren in the Pinners' Hall from 26 November 22 Edward IV [1482]. William Parker and Robert Howton have received of the wife of John Plays, on whose soul may God have mercy, on behalf of the craft in money £3 5s. 10d.
Item they have received of the brothers and sisters of the craft in quarterage for the second year, that is the first year of the reign of King Richard III [1483–1484] total 19s.
Item received of John Randolf for house rent 7s.
Sum of receipts £4 11s. 10d.

26. [f. 32] The parcels of the costs and expenses [incurred] during the term of the wardens and umpers
Payments
First for lime and sand 3d.
Item for a board 5d.
Item for nails 1d.
Item for the tiler and his man 9d.
Item for putting in a lock 1d.
Item for 3 roof tiles 3d.
Item for removing Richard Love from Ludgate 4d.
Item laid out for the cloth and staining thereof 5d.
Item for a dirge for John Plays 2s. 6d.
Item for a mass at the Whitefriars 16d.
Item for the sexton 2d.
Item for the Whitefriars on St James's day [25 July] for the brothers and sisters 2s. 6d.
Item paid to Thomas Payne[82] for Midsummer quarter 5s.
Item paid to Thomas Payne for Michaelmas quarter 5s.
Item paid for boat hire for the sheriffs 10d.
Item paid for boat hire for the mayor 10d.
Item delivered a yard cloth to John Stoneham 5s. 6d.
Item for the beadle's wages for 3 quarters 5s.
Item paid for the waxchandler 27s. 0½d.
Item paid for writing the account 12d.
Sum of payments 59s. 3d.

82. Thomas Payne, carpenter, originally leased the tenement used as Pinners' Hall from the Taylors' company and then sublet it to the Pinners.

27. [f. 32v.] Be it remembered that William Parker and Robert Howton, wardens of the craft, on 25 November 1 Richard III [1483], after the accounts had been presented to the brethren in the hall of the craft, the aforesaid, now late, wardens [left] the craft with £5 12s. 5d.

28. [f. 33] The account of William Machon, umper, John Bartlet and John Wekys, wardens of the craft, made their accounts before the brethren in the Pinners' Hall [forthe period] from 25 November 1483 to 26 November 1487
Receipts
First of Robert Rumbold's wife 20s.
Item of William Leche 13s. d
Item of the *mylpecker*[83] 7d.
Item of Kaward 21d.
Item of quarterage for 4 years £3 9s. 6d.
Item received of the brethren for our suit at Westminster in the days of King Richard 6s. 4d.
Item received of [Richard] Halamshyre rent for 4 years £4.
Item received of [John] Stoneham and [Richard] Brysbe 8d.
Sum of receipts £9 12s. 2d.

29. [f. 33v.] The parcels of the costs and expenses of the umper and wardens during their term of office
First paid for repairs in the hall 6s. 3d.
Item paid to the beadle 20d.
Item paid for assembling divers times at the Cutlers' Hall 4d.
Item paid for the craft's suit at Westminster 8s. 8d.
Item paid for a bill of plea for the craft 3s.
Item paid for a supplication 4s.
Item paid for a bill 3s. 4d.
Item paid for 2 indentures for the craft 16d.
Item paid 3 years' rent to Thomas Payne £4.
Item paid to the Whitefriars for 4 trentals, each trental 2s. 6d. 10s.
Item to the singers for 4 years 5s. 4d.
Item to the sexton for 4 years 16d.
Item paid for a trental for Thomas Wakelyn 2s. 6d.
Item paid to the plumber for mending the gutter 16d.
Item paid to the tiler and his man 8s. 4d.
Item for 10 sacks of lime 20d.
Item for a load of sand 6d.
Item for a faggot ½d.
Item for 1,000 tiles 5s.
Item for 13 roof tiles 7d.
Item paid to [Richard] Halamshyre for taking away rubbish and other labour 2s. 5d.

83. Mill-picker: one who fashions the grinding surfaces of millstones.

Item to John Stoneham for washing and quarterage 22d.
[f. 34] Item paid for a boat with 4 oars at the coming of King Richard [III] 3s. 4d.
Item paid for making a bill to fairs[84] 2d.
Item paid to the beadle at midsummer for a whole year 5s.
Item paid for a boat to Westminster with the sheriffs several times 4s.
Item paid to the waxchandler as appears by bill 19s. 11d.
Item for writing this account 12d.
Sum of all payments £9 2s. 10½d.

30. Be it remembered that William Machon, umper, John Bartlet and John Wekys, wardens of the craft, after the presentation of accounts to the brethren assembled in the Pinners' Hall on 25 November 1487, the wardens then received, on behalf of the craft, from William Machon, late umper, John Bartlet and John Wekys, late wardens £6 1s. 9½d.
Item the said wardens gave to the box for a reward 20s.
Sum of all £7 1s. 9½d.

31. [f. 34v.] Be it remembered that, in the aforesaid year, there remains in the hall the following stuff
In primis 2 tablecloths (*tablers*) of maiden heads and scallop shell
A tablecloth of cross diamonds [crossed out]
Item a towel and 2 plain table cloths
Item a linen bag
Item 3 dozen platters 3 dozen dishes and 20 [gap]
Item 3 dozen saucers.
Item a table of the brotherhood
Item a little coffer and a box
Item a latten basin with a new [gap]
[Different hand] Item a banner of changeable sarsenet with an image of St James and a maiden head and scallop shells given by William Parker, pinner
Item a banner of red buckram with a maiden head with scallop shells
Item a pall of blue buckram lined with linen and 4 scutcheons thereto
[Different hand] Item 2 plain tablecloths and a towel of diaper and a plain [one]
Item 6 napkins of diaper
Item a basin and a ewer
Item 2 torches - [in another hand] they be sold to the use of the fellowship
Item a table cloth [given] by Christopher Jeffrey of diaper and crossed diamonds

32. [f. 35] The account of William Parker, upper warden, Robert Ettell and Richard Tweke, wardens of the craft, who gave their account in the Pinners' Hall 1 August 1490

84. i.e a bill about travelling to fairs. See Barron, *London in the Later Middle Ages*, pp. 81–2, and Anne F. Sutton, 'The shop-floor of the London Mercery Trade, c. 1200-c.1500', *Nottingham Medieval Studies*, 45 (2001) pp. 12–50, esp. p. 37.

Paid to [Thomas] Payne for 7 quarters for house rent 35s.
Paid to Richard Appulby for 3 years' wages 15s.
Paid for a supplication to the mayor 20d.
Item paid to [Robert] Danyell for divers summonses for our supplication 2s.
Paid for the enrolling of the same supplication 2s.
Paid to Richard Machon for pursuing the same supplication 12d.
Paid to an officer for 3 summons for Richard Grene 12d.
Paid to an officer of the Chamber for warning the foreigns 8d.
Paid for cleaning an image 2d.
Paid to the sexton of the friars 4d.
Paid to the singers at the mass 12d.
Paid to the prior of the friars for 3 trentals 7s. 6d.
Paid to the singers for the mass 16d.
Paid to the sexton 4d.
Paid to the singers of the mass 12d.
Paid for cleaning the candlestick 1d.
[f. 35v.] Paid for writing the aforesaid supplication 22d.
Paid to the chandler for setting up the light 2d.
Paid to the waterman for a boat to Westminster with the sheriffs 12d.
Paid for making an indenture for the tenement of the hall 12d.
Paid to the master of the Taylors for making clean the figures (*fegres*) 16s. 8d.
Paid for a boat to Westminster 7d.
Paid for a labourer for 4 days 20d.
Paid to a carpenter for timber as appears by bill 9s. 5 d.
Paid for 9 sacks of lime 18d.
Paid for straw and *moty*[85] 4d.
Paid to a dauber for 5½ days 3s. 8d.
Paid for a load of loam 13d.
Paid for taking away the rubbish 22½d.
Paid to the carpenter for timber 9s.
Paid to carpenter and dauber and labourers, lime and sand as appears by bill 32s. 2 ½d.
Paid for chisel (*preke*) and nails and irons and loam 25s. 4d.
Paid to Thomas Boyle, waxchandler, for wax and making, as appears by bill 14s. 6½d.
Paid to Robert for repairs 27s. 3½d.
Also paid for writing this account 12d.
Sum total paid £10 19s. 5d.

33. [f. 36.] The receipts of William Parker, Robert Ettell and Richard Tweke
received of Richard Halamshyre for 2 years and a quarter 45s.

85. Pigment, see **23** above.

Received of Robert [corrected to Nicholas] Batte for his freedom 20s.
Received of William Beaumont for a fine 10d.
Received of Richard Brysbe, a fine 10d.
Received of Richard Brysbe to be a brother 3s. 4d.
Received of Richard Halamshyre to be a brother 20d.
Received of William Thomson in part payment for his presenting 15d.
Received on St Paul's day[86] of John Matson in part payment to be a brother 12d.
Received of William Castell to be a brother 3s. 4d.
Paid to Thomas Boyle, waxchandler, to his man for setting up the light 2d.
Received of Thomas Ellys for a fine 20d.
Received for quarterage for 3 years 56s. 6d.
Received of Thomas Rollenson to be a freeman 10s.
Received of Thomas Boyle, waxchandler, for 3 years' quarterage 3s.
Sum total received £7 8s. 5d.
There rests in William Parker's hands, all things reckoned and paid, 2 August [1490] £3 10s. 10½d.

34. [f. 36v blank: f. 37.]
The account of William Parker, upper warden, Robert Ettell and John Stoneham, wardens of the craft, made their account before the brethren in the Pinners' Hall on 1 August 1490 until [15 December 1491].
Receipts
First, received of the wardens of the Daubers (*dubbers*) for making a supper in the hall 16d.
Item received of Robert Chenwyth, 25 February, for his wife to be a sister 20d.
Item of Nicholas Batte for 2 years' quarterage 12d.
Item received of Richard Halamshyre for Michaelmas and Christmas quarterage 10s.
Item received of Robert Chenwyth's wife as a gift to the box 20d.
Item received of Robert Danyell for quarterage for the year passed 6d.
Item received of James Purdon to be a freeman 10s.
Received at the last account in the hands of William Parker, Robert Ettell and Richard Quycke for Robynson's fine 3s. 4d.
Item received of William Browne to be a brother 3s. 4d.
[f. 37v.] Item received of Richard Beaumont for the year past 6d.
Item received of Everard Newlyn to be a brother 3s. 4d.
Item received of Alice Hemmysley to be a sister 3s. 4d.
Item received in quarterage for the whole year 16s.
Sum Total 56s.

86. See above, **15**, n. 75 .

35. Payments
First paid for a boat to Westminster with the sheriffs 1490 12d.
Item paid for a boat to Westminster with the mayor 12d.
Item paid to a sergeant of the mayor's for a search 20d.
Paid to John Hall sergeant, for going with the wardens on the search 12d.
Paid to Richard Appulby, 3 June, for his year's wages 5s.
Paid to the Whitefriars on St James's day [25 July] for a trental 2s. 6d.
Paid to a mayor's sergeant for sending John White to the mayor twice 2s.
[f. 38] Paid to a sheriff's sergeant for arresting John White 8d.
Paid for actions [against] the said John [White] 6d.
Paid for mending the table 4d.
Paid for a boat to bring the sheriffs to Westminster 12d.
Paid for a boat to bring the mayor to Westminster 5d.
Paid to Thomas Payne 1490 [rent] 20s.
Paid to the said [Thomas] Payne 1491 10s.
Paid for burying Robert Hill's wife, 22 September 1490, and for making 2 torches weighing 47 pounds at a ½d. per lb. Sum 23½d.
Item the waste of the torches 6d.
Item to tapers of 16 pounds 9½d.
Item for the burial of Robert Chenwyth's wife and for the making of 4 torches weighing 86lbs. at ½d. [per lb.] 3s. 7d.
Item in waste of the torches 3 lbs. 18d.
For making of 4 tapers weighing 40 lbs. 20d.
[f. 38v.] waste ½ lb. 4d.
Item 2 *prickets* [candles] of 1 lb. on St James's day [25 July] 1491 8d.
Sum total 10s. 6d. as appears by a bill
Paid to Robert Ettell for washing and scouring the cloths and vessels of the hall for 4 years 2s.
Paid to a clerk for writing this account and writing of divers bills 14d.
Sum total £3 0s. 9d.
15 December 1491, all things being accounted for, William Parker, Robert Ettell and John Stoneham left in the hands of John Bartlet, John Wekys and John Stoneham £3 9s. 10d.
Be it remembered that Richard Halamshyre owes, at the following Christmas after this account, for the whole year of 1491 20s.

36. [f. 39] John Bartlet, upper warden, John Wekys and [John] Stoneham, wardens of the craft, gave these accounts in the Pinners' Hall 10 September 1492.
In primis received of Agnes Bartlet 28s.
Item received of quarterage 17s.
Item received of Richard Halamshyre for rent for the past quarter on Our Lady day [25 March] 1491 5s.
Item received for Midsummer quarter following 1491 6s.
Item received for Michaelmas quarter following 4s.
Sum [receipts] £3.

37. Payments
Item paid for a trental for John Bartlet 2s. 6d.
Item paid for a trental for John Stoneham 2s. 6d.
Item paid for a trental for all the brothers and sisters on St James's day [25 July] 2s. 6d.
Item delivered to the [White]friars as a reward on St James's day 12d.
Item for making the hall clean 2d.
Item for making 2 pipe keys 8d.
Item paid the beadle a half year's wages 2s. 6d.
Item paid for writing this account 6d.
Item paid the waxchandler as appears by bill 18s. 6¼d.
Sum total 30s. 10d.
[f. 39v.] Note that Richard Halamshyre owes to the craft of Pinners for three quarters past at Midsummer 1492
Note that Agnes Bartlet owes the craft 12s. 10d.
There rests in this account in clear money 59s. 2d. which we delivered in the whole body of the craft to William Machon 57s. 4d.

38. [f. 40] The account of William Machon, upper warden, John Wekys and Robert Ettell, wardens of the craft, laid before the brethren in Pinners' Hall, [for the period] 10 September 1492 to 3 December 1495.
In primis received by the whole body of the craft on the first day 57s. 4d.
Item received of Agnes Ettell to be a sister 20d.
Item received of Richard Halamshyre, at divers times, that he owed before our time 20s.
Item received of the said Richard at St Peter's day [1 August] 1493 2s.
Item received of the said Richard at St Thomas's day next [29 December] 2s.
Item received by the hands of William Parker 15 July 1493 5s.
Item received of Richard Halamshyre 9 August 1493 12d.
Item received of the said Richard at Michaelmas, for a whole year's past rent when he was made freeman 1493 10s.
Item received of Laurence Baker when he was made freeman 10s.
Item received of Skynner's wife for a fine 4d.
[f. 40v.] Item received for 4 fines for 4 distraints because they would not come at the summoning 15d.
Item received of Richard Halamshyre for the quarters of Our Lady and Midsummer 1494 10s.
Item received for 2 years' quarterage 37s.
Sum total £7 17s. 7d.

39. Payments
First paid for a boat to go with the mayor to Westminster 5d.
Item paid to Richard Stafford Saint Nicholas day [6 December] 1492 2s. 6d.
Item paid to Robert Skydmore, the beadle, 11 February, for a half year's wages from Candlemas [2 February] to Lammas [1 August] 2s. 6d.

Item paid to the stationer for the setting to the table 3d.
Item paid for the mass on St James's day to the Whitefriars 12d.
Item paid for a trental of masses at Whitefriars 2s. 6d.
Item paid to Thomas Payne, carpenter, for a year's rent past before my time, as appears by acquittance by the hand of Dygley[87] 20s.
Item paid to the warden of the Taylors for the past quarter at Midsummer, 10 August 1493 5s.
[f. 41] Paid to Richard Smith,[88] warden of the Taylors, for the past quarter's rent at Michaelmas 5s.
Item paid to Richard Smith, warden of the Taylors for the Christmas quarter 5s.
Item paid to Robert Skydmore, for Lammas to Candlemas 2s. 6d.
Item paid to the wardens of the Taylors, for the quarter of Our Lady, 22 June 1494 5s.
Item paid for 2 trental masses on St James's day [25 July] 1494 5s.
Item paid for prayers for the brothers and sisters of the Pinners 2s. 6d.
Item paid to the singers on the same day 12d.
Item paid to the sexton for lighting the candle 4d.
Item paid to Robert Kelham, warden of the Taylors, 18 September 1494 for midsummer quarter 5s.
Item paid to Robert Skydmore for his year's wages at Candlemas 1494 5s.
Item lent at the same time to Robert Skydmore, on [pledge of] a ring, in part payment for the next year 2s.
Item paid to Robert Kelham, warden of the Taylors, for Michaelmas quarter 5s.
Item paid Robert Kelham, warden of the Taylors for Christmas quarter and the following quarter of Our Lady 10s.
Item paid on St James's day for a trental of masses at the Whitefriars for the brothers and sisters 1495 2s. 6d.
[f. 41v.] Item paid to the sexton for trimming (*sparyng*) the lights 2d.
Item paid for a boat to Westminster with Master Somer[89] 6d.
Item paid for a trental for Isabel Vicary 2s. 6d.
Item paid to Thomas Boyle, waxchandler, for the past 2 years 25s. 6d.
Item paid to John Herste, warden of the Taylors, for the 2 past quarters, Midsummer and Michaelmas 1495 10s.
Item paid to Robert Ettell for washing and scouring 12d.
Item paid for writing this account 8d.
Sum total £6 11s.
Memorandum of the debts owed to the craft

87. Probably Richard Dyngley, warden of the Merchant Taylors 1492–3, see Matthew Davies ed., *The Merchant Taylors' Company of London: Court Minutes 1486–1493* (Stamford, 2000), p. 289.
88. Richard Smith was elected one of the four wardens of the Taylors' Company in June 1493. He was given special responsibility for collecting the income from the company's lands and tenements. He became Master of the company in 1502: see Davies, *The Merchant Taylors' Company of London*, pp. 253–255, 301.
89. Henry Somer, haberdasher, sheriff 1495–6.

Item Agnes Bartlet owes 12s. 10d.
Item Richard Halamshyre, at this day as appears in this book at the coming Christmas 1495 30s.
Item Robert Skydmore owes on a ring 2s.
Rests in the box 26s. 4d.

40. [f. 42] The account of William Parker, upper warden, Robert Ettell [the rest of this page remains blank]
[f. 42v.] The account of William Parker, upper warden, Robert Ettell and Robert Chenwyth, wardens, who made their account to the craft in the Pinners' Hall 20 April 1497.
In primis received by the whole body of the craft at the last account 26s. 4d.
Received of Richard Halamshyre in part payment of his old debts 17s.
Received of Richard Brysbe for failure to appear 2d.
Received of Goodman of the Chequers (*Checyz*) in Fleet Street for setting foreigns to work 10d.
Received of John Ross to be a freeman 6s. 8d.
Received of John Wright to be made a freeman 5s.
Received of the fellowship in aid of the plea as appears by bill 15s. 4d.
Received of Nicholas Horner for a fine to the Chamber 8d.
Received of Thomas Michell to be a brother 3s. 4d.
Received of Thomas, Master Brown's[90] man, in part payment to be made a freeman 3s. 4d.
[f. 43.] Received in quarterage 15s.
Sum total £4 13s. 8d.
[Payments]
Paid to a yeoman of the Chamber for sending John Alsop to the Chamberlain 4d.
Paid for searching in the mayor's court for a writ of *requisitione scire*[91] 2d.
Paid for a burden of rushes 1½d.
Paid to the clerk of the Chamber for the search of Robert Cadman 4d.
Paid to a yeoman of the Chamber for sending [for] John Ross 4d.
Paid to [John] Hall, the sergeant, for a search 20d.
Paid to the Whitefriars for a trental 2s. 6d.
Paid to the friars for singing on the same day 12d.
Paid, 28 January, to Robert Skydmore for the whole of his wages for last year 1496 5s.
Paid for a boat to go with the sheriffs to Westminster 6d.
[f. 43v.] Paid for a quarter of coals 5d.
Paid at Michaelmas the rent for our hall for the whole of the past year 1496 20s.
Paid for the Christmas quarter and Our Lady's quarter 10s.
Paid for carrying the stuff out of the hall 2d.

90. Probably William Browne, mercer, sheriff 1492–3, mayor 1507–8.
91. *Requisitione scire*: a written enquiry into the circumstances of a case.

41. The costs of the plea between the Pinners and the Wiremongers
In primis paid to Master More[92] for the *scire facias*:[93] 2 payments 3s. 4d.
Paid to Master Town Clerk[94] for entering the *requisitione scire* 2s.
Paid to the attorney twice 2s.
Paid for making the *scire facias* 8d.
Paid for administering the plea 4d.
Paid for the copy of the plea 8d.
Paid for the continuation 3 times 6d.
Paid for a bill to put in the plea 4d.
Paid to John Hall as a reward 12d.
Paid for making the supplication 3s. 4d.
Paid to Master Town Clerk for putting up the supplication 15d.
[f 44.] Paid to Yoner 12d.
Paid to a scrivener for making the later bill 3d.
Paid for a pickerel for Master Chamberlain[95] 16d.
Paid to the clerk for entering the ordinances in the town clerk's book 20d.
Paid for entering of the enrolling in the [London] Letter book L[96] 20d.
Paid to Giles [clerk in the Mayor's court] for the copy of the ordinance 15d.
Paid to John Hall, sergeant, for the search at Bartholomew's ordinary fair 20d.
Paid to Master Chamberlain for a fine 13s. 4d.
Paid to Master Town Clerk for his fee. 3s. 4d.
Paid to a carter for carrying a load of rubbish 2d.
Paid for cleaning the hall 4d.
Paid for *rosses* [roses?] 2d.
Paid for writing this account 8d.
Paid for board and nails 6d.
Sum total £4 6s. 1½d.
Rests in the box 7s. 6½d.

[This is the last entry of the pinners before they amalgamated with the wiredrawers and became jointly the wiresellers]

42. [f. 44v.] In this, the 12th year of King Henry VII [1496–1497] in the box after the fellowship of the wiresellers made their account there remained 10s.

92. Probably [Sir] John More, at this time a lawyer in Lincoln's Inn, and the father of Thomas More.
93. *Scire facias*: a judicial writ which requires the persons against whom it is brought to repeal a record: in this case, the existing ordinances of the two companies as the preliminary to the creation of a new one by amalgamation of the pinners and the wiredrawers to form the wiresellers.
94. Nicholas Packenham, common/town clerk 1490–1510.
95. William Milbourne, painter, chamberlain 1492–1506.
96. *LBL*, pp. 319–321, **65**, **66**.

This is the account of William Parker, upper warden, Ralph Underwood and William Blank, wiresellers, from 20 April 12 Henry VII [1497] to Our Lady Day, the Assumption [15 August] of the same year
First received at their account 10s.
Item received of Richard Halamshyre for quarterage 6d.
Item received of John Wright in part payment for his freedom 12d.
Item received of Nicholas Horner to be a brother 3s. 4d.
Item received a year's quarterage 31s. 9d.
Sum total 46s. 7d.

43. [f. 45] Memorandum for the plea of Thomas Hill
First of William Parker 3s. 4d.
Item of Ralph Underwood 2s.
Item of William Blank 12d.
Item of William Machon 12d.
Item of [John] Alsop 20d.
Item of Robert Cadman 20d.
Item of Robert Ettell 20d.
Item of Thomas Michell 20d.
Item of John Freman 20d.
Item of William Frebrige 20d
Item of William Wiles 8d.
Item of Lewis Gryffyn 8d.
Item of Thomas Rawlyn 8d.
Item of Robert Chenwyth 4d.
Item of Henry Vulvyn' 4d.
Item of John Ross 12d.
Item of John Wekys 12d.
Item of Richard Brysbe 8d.
Item of Richard Stafford 6d.
Item of John Mason 4d.
Item of William Jones 2d.
Item of Roger Ussher 4d.
Item of Christopher Pursell 2d.
Item of Richard Beaumont 6d.
Item of Thomas Arnold 2d.
Item of John Bedill 3d.
Item of John Wright 2d.
[f. 45v.] Item of John Thorp 2d.
Item of Nicholas Shernell 2d.
Item of Nicholas Horner 2d.
Item of John Aleyn 2d.
Sum 25s. 11d.
Sum of all the receipts £3 12s. 6d.

44. The parcels laid out for Thomas Hill in the Commissary Court[97]
First for entering the plaint 2d.
Item paid to the summoner 4d.
Item paid to Master Rede[98] to be attorney 3s. 4d.
Item paid to Master Rede's clerk, for making a bill 2d.
Item paid to the summoner for summoning St Benet's parish 8d.
Item paid for a quart of wine for the Commissary 2d.
Item paid for Master Rede 8 July 3s. 4d.
Item paid to the scribe 12 July 12d.
Item paid to the scrivener the same day 12d.
Item paid to the summoner for calling Thomas Hill at the same time 4d.
[f. 46] Item paid into the hands of Ralph Underwood for performing the plea 4d.
Item for fetching of the articles of the plea 4d.
Item paid to the Commissary on 15 July for the following of 3 *cominecat*[*es*] 20s.
Item paid to the scribe for writing them at the same time 2s. 4d.
Item paid for serving the 3 *cominecat*[*es*] 2s.
Item paid to Master Rede's man on 19 July for taking the names of the records the day Thomas Hill was pardoned 12d.
Item paid to the scribe on the same day for taking the names of the same records 6d.
Item paid for the costs of fellowship on that day 6d.
Item paid for going to Lambeth 4d.
Sum 19s. 6d.

45. The payments of the wardens of the Wiresellers
First paid to Thomas Joyner, for amending a bill from the search 8d.
Item paid to Prudefoot for fetching in of the same into the [London] Letter Book L 16d.
[f. 46v.] Item paid to Thomas Joyner for entering the same in the book of Master Town Clerk 16d.
Item paid to Giles for entering into our ordinary 4d.
Item for parchment 1d.
Item paid the mayor's sergeant, 31 May, for a search 18d.
Item paid the mayor's sergeant for half a day's search 8d.
Item paid to the beadle, Robert Skydmore, on 21 June for his wages 2s.
Item paid for half a quarter of cloth for the livery 6d.
Item paid for 500 sprig nails 3d.
Item paid for half a quartron[99] of roof nails 2d.
Item for a hundred of *sap laths* 4d.

97. For this court see Robert Wunderli, *London Church Courts and Society on the Eve of the Reformation* (Medieval Academy of America, 1981), pp. 10–15.
98. Bartholomew Rede, goldsmith, sheriff 1497–8.
99. A measure used for commodities other than liquids.

Item for a load and a half of loam 6d.
Item for half a load of sand 3d.
Item for a dauber and his man for 5 days 5s. 5d.
Item for a dozen of red lead 20d.
Item paid for nails 1½d.
Item for coal 1½d.
Item for faggots 1d.
Item paid for 9 sacks of lime 16d.
Item for carrying 3 loads of rubbish 6d.
Item paid for 2 loads of rushes 3d.
Item paid a dauber for half a day 4d.
Item paid for writing this account 8d.
Item paid for washing cloths 2d.
[f. 47] Item for coal ½d.
Item for scouring the candlesticks 3d.
Item paid to Whitefriars for a trental of masses 2s. 6d.
Item paid to the sexton 2d.
Item paid for the mayor's sergeant for Roger Ussher 8d.
Item paid for a hundred of *sap laths* 4d. [crossed out]
Item paid for 2 quarters of oak 3d.
Item paid for 3 legs for the grate 1½d.
Item paid for workmanship of all this 4d.
Item paid to Robert Skydmore 25 August for the past Midsummer quarter 20d.
Item paid to Robert Skydmore on the same day for faggots and water at our court 4d.
Item paid on the same day to Robert Skydmore for scouring the vessels 10d.
Item paid to the same Robert for a quarter of coals 4d.
Item paid for water 3d.
Item paid for a quarter of oak to go over the hall 3d.
Item paid to Thomas Boyle as appears by his bill 10s. 10d.
Item paid in rent for the hall for the Midsummer quarter 5s.
Sum 44s. 6d.
Sum of all the payments £3 4s. 11d.

46. [f. 47v.] Memorandum that Robert Ettell, Ralph Underwood and Robert Cadman, wardens of the wiresellers, on 24 August 13 Henry VII [1497], paid to Mynton, sergeant of the mayor, as appears by their account for a search 12d.
Item [taken] at the same search of Robert Cloney 18,500 pins
Item taken from Richard Stafford at the same search 1000 pins
Item taken from Roger Ussher at the same search 2000 pins
Item taken of Lewis Gryffyn at the same search 1000 pins
Item taken of Wayt's wife at the same search 2000 pins
Item taken of Halthrop at the same search 2850 pins
Item taken of John Lokle, foreign, at the same search 1000 pins

Item paid to Mynton, the sergeant, for a search made within the city 14 Henry VII [1498–1499] 12d.

47. [f. 48] The account of Robert Ettell, upper warden, Robert Cadman and Ralph Underwood, wardens of the craft of wiresellers, made their account before the craft in the Wiresellers Hall in 1499
First paid for a banner of the Assumption of Our Lady and St Clement with anchors[100] and scallop shells 10s.
Item paid for an image of St Clement 15s.
Item paid for wax and resin for the same image 1d.
Item paid for a cord (*lasse*) to fasten the anchor by 1d.
Item paid to the Whitefriars for fetching out our Bull 8d.
Item paid for 3 banner staves 3s. 4d.
Item paid to the scrivener for the indenture between Thomas Boyle and us 4d.
Item paid to John Ross for barge hire when going with the mayor to Westminster 3s. 4d.
[f. 48v.] Item paid to the same John Ross as a reward, by the will of the company 12d.
Item paid the following year for barge hire to bring the sheriffs to Westminster 6s. 8d.
Item for rushes to the same barge 2d.
Item paid for barge hire in the same year to bring the mayor to Westminster 6s. 8d.
Item for rushes to the same barge 2d.
Item paid to the rent gatherer for the Taylors for Midsummer and Michaelmas quarters 10s.
Item paid to the wardens of the Taylors, 21 June, for the farm of our hall, gathered from the company 10s.
Item paid to the wardens of the Taylors for Midsummer and Michaelmas quarter rent, collected from the company towards the 10s. required 5s. 8d.
Item Robert Ettell paid to make up the sum of 10s. 4s. 4d.
Item paid to the wardens of the Taylors for the quarters of Christmas and Our Lady day which was received from the kilderkin[101] of ale that [William] Frebrige gave towards the same rent 6s.
Item that Robert Ettell paid to make up the deficit of 10s. 10s.
[f. 49] Item paid to Robert Skydmore for 2 years' wages 13s. 4d.

48. Memorandum that I Robert Ettell, Ralph Underwood and Robert Cadman, wardens of the Wiresellers have in 13 Henry VII [1497–1498] paid to Mynton, the Mayor's sergeant, for a search at St Bartholomew's fair 12d.
Item paid a yeoman of the Chamber to send for John Wekys 4d.

100. St Clement I, Pope, was martyred by drowning with an anchor and chains attached to him. He became the patron saint of metal workers.
101. 18 gallon cask

Item paid to a yeoman of the Chamber to send for William Blanke 4d.
Item for fetching out a testimonial from the Official's court 12d.
Item paid to Master Rede for the plea between us and Thomas Hill 20d.
Item paid to Master Scheffeld[102] for the same plea for his advice 20d.
Item paid for a quarter of Rumsey which was sent to Master Commissary 4d.
Item paid for the wine for the scribe and the company 4d.
[f. 49v] Item paid to the scribe for the examination of Thomas Freman 18d.
Item paid for the examination of Thomas Rawlyn 9d.
Item paid for the examination of [John] Worsop 9d.
Item paid for the examination of John Alsop 9d.
Item paid for nails to nail the windows at the hall 3d.
Item paid to amend our writing 16d.
Item paid to Robert Skydmore for bearing the image of St Clement to the Whitefriars 2d.
Item to Joan Skydmore, servant, for helping at the hall 1d.
Item paid to the writer of our correspondence (*thynges*) 2d.
Item paid to a scribe for the copy of our plea 2s. 8d.
Item a reward to the scribe and the clerk for letting us have the copy of the plea quickly 8d.
Item paid to a clerk for writing a roll of the quarterages 2d.
Item paid to a doctor for our plea between us and Thomas Hill 3s. 4d.
Item Robert Cadman has paid Master Scheffeld for his counsel on the same plea 20d.
[f. 50] Item paid to the scribe for entering the copies of our plea when Master Doctor was there 2d.
Item paid to Master Rede for his counsel 20d.
Item paid to a summoner to send for Thomas Hill 4d.
Item paid for entering of the decree in the presence of Master Doctor, Master Scheffeld and Master Rede 4d.
Item paid to a summoner to summon Thomas Hill to [answer] the same decree 4d.
Item to a clerk to draw a bill of our costs between Thomas Hill and us 2d.
Item paid to a summoner to call Thomas Hill to his decree [before] the company at the instance of Master Scheffeld 4d.
Item paid to our Doctor 3s. 4d.
Item paid to Master Rede our man of counsel on the same day 3s. 4d.
Item paid for entering our proctor and for summoning Thomas Hill before the Commissary 4d.
Item paid to Master Scheffeld for his counsel 20d.
Item paid for the continuance of our plea when the two Doctors met before the Commissary 2d.

102. [Sir] Robert Sheffield, recorder of London 1496–1508.

Item paid by the hand of Ralph Underwood upon St Bride's eve[103] for an act made when the eight Doctors were there 2d.

49. [f. 50v.] Item paid to our Doctor, by the hand of Ralph Underwood, on St Bride's day, for his counsel 3s. 4d.
Item paid to [John] Worsop scrivener, for making our word on St Blaise's day [3 February] 2s.
Item paid to Master Scheffeld, our man of counsel, by hand of Ralph Underwood on the same day 20d.
Item paid to the writer of our parcels 2d.
Item paid by the hand of Ralph Underwood to the scribe for writing out two acts in the court before Master Scheffeld 6d.
Item paid to a notary for making an award by instrument 4s. Robert Ettell has paid the one half and Ralph Underwood the other half
Item for Master Scheffeld and the Company to drink 5d.
Item paid for half a bushel of coal and to Robert Skynner for making a fire when the Company were together 1d.
Item paid for a key to the store house door 3d.
Item paid for a quarter of coals 5d.
[f. 51] Item paid to Giles, clerk of my Lord the Mayor's court, for an act of my Lord's court, brought before the Commissary 16d.
Item paid to the Whitefriars for a trental for Richard Quycke 2s. 6d.
Item paid for an instrument to bring before the Commissary 3s. 4d.
Item at the deposit of this instrument for the act 2d.
Item paid to John Worsop for making our supplication to Master Purchase, Mayor of London[104] 17d.
Item paid to Master Pagnam[105] our man of counsel 3s. 4d.
Item paid to a yeoman of the Chamber to send for Thomas Hill 4d.
Item paid for 2 pikes 9s.
Item paid for 2 gallons of wine 16d.
Item paid to John Worsop for amending our award by the instrument 14d.
Item paid for going over the water to Paris garden[106] for our pikes 1d.
Item paid to a yeoman of the Chamber to send for Thomas Hill 4d.
Item paid for setting in of our instrument in our award 14d.
Item paid to the yeoman for sending old [John] Blanche and his son to the Chamberlain and from there to the Counter 12d.

50. [f. 51v.] Item paid to Master Rede's clerk, for an act made to bring before the judge at Paul's Chain[107] 12d.
Item paid for a pottel of wine given to Master Scheffeld and his wife 4d.

103. St Bride was a synonym for St Bridget whose feast day was 1 February. A number of pinners appear to have lived in Fleet Street, in the parish of St Bride.
104. William Purchase, mercer, mayor of London 1497–8.
105. Probably Nicholas Packenham, common clerk.
106. In Southwark, see M. Carlin, *Medieval Southwark* (London , 1996) pp. 31–2.
107. Paul's Chain was the name of the street leading south out of the Cathedral precinct.

Item paid to a yeoman of the Chamber for sending twice for Thomas Kyngslond 8d.
Item paid to a yeoman of the Chamber for sending for Robert Blowman 4d.
Item paid to a yeoman of the Chamber for sending for William Boower, the clerk 4d.
Item to send the same yeoman for [John] Doly 4d.
Item paid to the same yeoman of the Chamber to bring the said John Doly to the Counter 4d.
Item paid to a yeoman of the Chamber for sending for John Gryffyn the elder 4d.
Item paid to Master Scheffeld our man of counsel for his [advice] 2s.
Item paid to a yeoman of the Chamber for sending for Master Bullesdone[108] to the Chamberlain 4d.
Item paid to a yeoman of the Chamber on the morrow following sending for Master Passmore[109] and Master Bullesdone to Master Chamberlain 4d.
[f. 52] Item paid the same day to these gentlemen for the making of the obligation in which we are bound with Thomas Hill 4d.
Item paid the same day in expenses to these gentlemen 18d.
Item paid to John Worsop for making a bill of our charges to show to the arbitrators (*dayesmen*) 8d.
Item for expenses of bread and ale for Master Chamberlain and Master Passmore at the Guildhall 2d.
Item paid for a copy for our selves 2d.
Item paid for 2 obligations of an award between Thomas Hill and us 8d.
Item paid to Master Rede for his fee 20d.
Item paid for wine for our Doctor 4d.
Item paid for ale at Master Passmore's when Master Chamberlain and Master Bullesdone were there 4d.
Item for washing the cloths that belong to the hall 8d.
Item paid the sexton for preparing our lights 4d.
Item paid to the [White]friars upon Our Lady's night for the good cheer they gave us at the drinking 4d.
Item paid to the friars the day after Our Lady's day for a trental for the brothers and sisters 2s. 6d.
Item paid to Master Grene, the Common Sergeant[110] 3s. 4d.
Item paid to John Worsop, scrivener, for entering our ordinary in our book 18d.
[f. 52v.] Item paid for paper to write more things at divers times 1d.
Item paid for washing the cloths that belong to the hall 8 pieces 4d.
Item paid for a bushel of coals when the Company was together 1d.

108. Thomas Bullesdone, skinner, who was elected as a warden of London Bridge in 1492.
109. John Pasmer, citizen and skinner, who was elected as a city auditor in 1491.
110. John Grene, common sergeant 1495–1521.

Paid to the Wardens of the Taylors for repairs to cellar in the hall, as shown by bill 3s.
Item paid to Robert Skydmore for cleaning the candlesticks 3d.
Item that Robert Ettell has paid for John Freman the [sum] which he granted for the rent of the hall 8d.
Item paid to Mynton, the sergeant of my Lord Mayor for a search in the 14th year of King Henry VII [1498–1499] 12d.
Item paid to the Whitefriars for a trental for the brothers and sisters 2s. 6d.
Item paid to the [White]friars, for the singers by the will of the Company as a reward 16d.
Item paid for a limner to set in our [t]able John Blanche the elder and Thomas Hill's wife 1d.
Item Robert Cadman paid towards the 40s. that was awarded to the arbitrators 12d.
Sum for parcels up to date £5 18s. 4d.

51. [f. 53] The award of the arbiters, Master Chamberlain, Master Passmore and Master Bullesdone was for us to bring in 40s.
Memorandum the whole Company paid towards the 40s.
Item received of William Parker 5s.
Item received of Robert Ettell 3s. 4d.
Item received of Robert Cadman 3s. 4d.
Item received of Ralph Underwood 20d.
Item received of William Machon 20d.
Item received of John Alsop 3s.
Item received of John Wekys 20d.
Item received of John Blanche 4d.
Sum 20s.
Item received of William Machon 12d.
Item received of Robert Chenwyth 8d.
Item received of Robert Ettell 20d.
Item received of William Parker 20d.
Item received of John Wekys 12d.
Item received of Lewis Gryffyn 4d.
Item received of Thomas Rawlyn 4d.
[f. 53v.] Item received of Robert Cadman 12d.
Item received of Richard Brysbe 4d.
Item received of John Alsop 12d.
Item received of William Frebrige 20d.
Item receieved of Thomas Michell 12d.
Item received of Ralph Underwood 3s. 4d.
Item received of Thomas Michell 12d.
Item received of John Ross 16d.
Item received of Harry Onwyn 8d..
Item received of Nicholas Horner 4d.
Item received of John Strode 4d.
Item received of John Alsop 4d.

Sum 19s.
Item paid to Thomas Boyle waxchandler for making our light and for the burial of Richard Quycke 18d.
Item paid for the making and writing out of our accounts 20d.
Memorandum this is the sum of payments made by Robert Ettell, Robert Cadman and Ralph Underwood [who] delivered the sum of £11 3s. 7d.

52. [f. 47] Memorandum that Robert Ettell has given a kilderkin of ale to the craft and those that gathered there, that is to say Thomas Rawlyn and Richard Glaston, raised 8s. 1 0d.
Memorandum that Master Parker gave a kilderkin of ale to the craft and the gatherers Lewis Gryffyn and Michael Wakelyn made thereof 9s.
Item John Alsop gave a dozen bread loaves to the same ale and Thomas Michell gave to the same ale 2 rounds of beef.
Memorandum that Robert Cadman gave a kilderkin of ale to the craft and the gatherers thereof were William Wyllys and John Wright who made of it 7s. 6d.
Memorandum that William Frebrige gave a kilderkin of ale to the craft and the gatherers thereof were John Ross and John Wright who made thereby 6s.
Item Ralph Underwood gave towards costs and charges 16d.
Item Robert Cadman has given towards costs and charges 12d.
Item received of Richard Burgeys in part payment of his quarterage 3d.
Item received of William Berell in part payment of his quarterage 3d.

53. Memorandum that this is the money gathered for the banner of St Clement and the image
First John Strode 2d.
[f. 54v.]
Item Ralph Wrytyll 4d.
Item Thomas Baten 2d.
Item William 2d.
Item William Wyllys 4d.
Item Nicholas Horner 4d.
Item Lewis Gryffyn 6d.
Item Walter Herst 1d.
Item David Wylliam 1d.
Item Bartholomew 1d.
Item John Barfote 1d.
Item Robert Canynge 1d.
Item Everard Newlyn 1d.
Item John Alyn 2d.
Item Richard Glaston 2d.
Item John Roo 2d.
Item William Elyot 2d.
Item Richard Page 2d.
Item John Wright 2d.

Item William Berell 2d.
Item Thomas Palmer 2d.
Item Richard Beaumont 2d.
Item for a sister 4d.
Item John Strode 4d.
Item Henry Dowbryche 2d.
[f. 55]
Item John Waryn 2d.
Item John Twenar 2d.
Item John Arnold 2d.
Item John Wekys 6d.
Item received of William Parker for Midsummer quarterage 5s.
Item received of the box 7s. 7d.

54. Memorandum that the brethren and the fellowship have given for the making of an image of St Clement on St Clement's day [23 November] as shown by the names following:
Item William Machon 4d.
Item John Wekys 12d.
Item Robert Chenwyth 2d.
Item William Wyllys 2d.
Item Lewis Gryffyn 2d.
Item Nicholas Horner 2d.
Item Thomas Arnold 2d.
Item Michael Waklyn 2d.
Item John Alyn 2d.
Item Nicholas Sarnayll 1d.
Item John Wright 2d.
Item Thomas Rawlyn 2d.
Item John Rawlyn of Stanley 18d.
Item John Strode 2d.
Item John Sewall 8d.
Item Thomas Kyngslond 4d.

55. [f. 55v.] Item received of the company for the plea between Thomas Hill and us 5s.
Item received of Anabel Page for past quarterage 12d.
Item received of William Machon 8d.
Item Robert Ettell 12d.
Item Robert Cadman 12d.
Item Ralph Underwood 12d.
Item William Parker 12d.
Item John Alsop 12d.
Item John Wekys 12d.
Item William Blank 6d.
Item Thomas Michell 8d.
Item William Frebrige 8d.
Item John Freman 4d.

Item William Wyllys 2d.
Item Lewis Gryffyn 2d.
Item received on 19 February for Richard Quycke's quarterage 4s.
Item received of John Ross 19 February to be a brother 3s.
Item received 20 June from the fellowship to pay the rent 10s.
Item received of John Mason for his quarterage 12d.
[f. 56] Item received of John Ross 8d.
Item received of John Berell for his quarterage 3d.
Item received of John Blanche the older for quarterage 3d.
Item received of Thomas Hill for his quarterage 3d.
Item received of Thomas Baten for the last payment for his freedom on Midsummer Day 20d.
Item received in quarterage 13 Henry VII [1497–1498] as appears by bill 40s. 6d.
Item received from Robert Thomlynson for his quarterage 2d.
Item received of Thomas Vynsent in part payment of this quarterage 4d.

56. These are the foreigns that have paid their fines in Robert Ettell's days, umper, Robert Cadman and Ralph Underwood, wardens of the Wiresellers
Item received of William Ingram for admission as a workman 20d.
Item received of David Wylliam for admission as a workman 20d.
Item received of Richard Hasyllhurst for admission as a workman 20d.
Item received of John Waryn for admission as a workman 20d.
[f. 56v.] Item received of Richard Wallwyn for admission as a workman 20d.
Item received of Thomas Brodwall for admission as a workman 20d.
Item received of Thomas Clarke for admission as a workman 20d.
Item received of George Constantyn for admission as a workman 20d.
Item received of William Etun, cardmaker, for admission as a workman 20d.
Item received of John Robynson for admission as a workman 20d.
Item received of Averey Constantyn for admission as a workman 20d.
Item received of Margaret Exnyng for admission as a work[wo]man 20d.
Item received of John Myryell in part payment for his freedom 6s. 8d.
Item received of John Petercam (*P*^{t}*cam*) from Bristol for admission as a workman 20d.
Item received of Richard Gowe for admission as a workman 20d.
[f. 57] Item received of Margaret Golde for admission as a workwoman 20d.
Item received of Margaret Crayford for admission as a workwoman 20d.
Item to admit Joan Fuller, [John] Alsop's servant, as a workwoman 20d.
Item John Bellingham for admission as a workman 20d.
Item Katherine Smyth for admission as a workwoman 20d.
Item received of Robert Stoke in part payment of his fine for admission as a workman 2s.

Item John Robynson for admission as a workman 20d.
Item Gehon Danyell for admission as a workwoman 20d.
Item received of William Kynge for admission as a workman 20d.
These are the foreigns who have paid their fines in the days of Robert Ettell, Ralph Underwood and Robert Cadman
[f. 57v.] Item received in quarterage 14 Henry VII [1498–1499] 50s.
Memorandum that these receipts of Robert Ettell, Robert Cadman and Ralph Underwood came to the sum of £11 10s. 11d.

57. This is the account of John Blanche, the umper, John Alsop and William Frebrige, wardens of the craft of Wiresellers in the year 1501.
[No further entries]

58.[f. 58] The account of John Wekys, umper warden, Thomas Michell and Thomas Rawlyn, wardens of the craft, made in the Wiresellers' Hall in 1504 in the 20th year of King Henry VII [1504–1505].
First paid for our hall in the Greyfriars for a half year 20d.
Item paid to the friars for all in the great masses 2d.
Item paid for barge hire at Michaelmas, bringing the sheriffs to Westminster 6s. 10d.
Item paid for barge hire to bring the mayor to Westminster in the same year 6s. 10d.
Item paid to Mynton, the sergeant, for going with us on our search for 2 days, 18 October 2s.
Item paid on these 2 days for meat and drink 3s. 6d
Item paid to the beadle at night, as appears by bill 2d.
[f. 58v.] Item paid to Thomas a Wod, carpenter, for making our scaffold when the prince came in[111] 5s. 1d.
And for the labourer for making the holes for the timber and for the stopping 2s. 2d.
Item paid to the carter for bringing our stuff from John Alsop, once 4d. and the second time 3d.
Item paid for the hanging up of our cloths and the stowing of our stuff 1d.
Item paid for a quarter of coals 5d.
Item paid for a *stapull* to the hall door 1d.
Item paid 3 times for coals 3d.
Item paid the beadle for his wages 10s.
Item paid the Whitefriars in the first year for a dirge and mass at night upon Our Lady day [25 March] and on the morrow the mass and for *erbyes* [herbs?] and the sexton 3s. 2d.

111. This probably refers to the civic reception for Prince Arthur and Catherine of Aragon in November 1502, see A.H. Thomas and I.D. Thornley, eds., *The Great Chronicle of London* (London, 1937), pp. 297–316, 447–8.

Item paid on the morrow after the session day for our breakfast at the Belle Sauvage[112] (*bell savage*) 2s.
Item paid to the beadle for his wages 5s.
Item paid to the waxchandler for 2 years 14s. 5d.
Item paid the second year at the Whitefriars for dirge and mass on the morrow 2s. 11d.

59. [f. 59] The receipts from quarterage:
Received John Wekys 3s.
Received Thomas Michell 3s.
Received Thomas Rawlyn 3s.
Received Robert Ettell 3s.
Received John Blanche 3s.
Received Robert Cadman 2s.
Received of William Frebrige 3s.
Received of John Alsop 1s.
Received of Ralph Underwood 3s.
Received of John Freman 6d.
Received of Robert Chenwyth 3s.
Received of John Mason 4d.
Received of John Ross 2d.
Received of William Blank 3d.
Received of Lewis Gryffyn 3s.
Received of William Wyllys 2s.
Received of Richard Brysbe 2s.
Received of new brothers to the company:
First of John Strode 40d.
Received for Joan, his wife 20d.
[f. 59v.] Received of Robert Blowman 40d.
Received of Thomas Baten 40d.
Received of John Attwattyre 40d.
Received of William Rogerrys , waxchandler 40d.
Received of John Adane and Alice his wife 5s.
The foreigns that paid their fines in the days of John Wekys, umper, Thomas Michell and Thomas Rawlyn, wardens:
Received of Edward Vahan to be a freeman among us 10s.
Received of John Green for admission as a workman 20d.
Received of Thomas Wadell for admission as a workman 20d.
Received of Ralph Morgon admitted [as a workman] 20d.
Received of Robert Stede for admission as a workman 20d.
Received of Laurence Smyth for admission as a workman 20d.
[f. 60] Received of the brethren for making the scaffold when the princess came[113]
Received of John Wekys 20d.
Received of Thomas Michell 20d.

112. Probably the inn on the north side of Fleet Street, between Fleet Bridge and Ludgate.
113. Probably Catherine of Aragon, see footnote 111.

Received of Thomas Rawlyn 20d.
Received of Robert Ettell 16d.
Received of John Blanche 12d.
Received of Robert Cadman 16d.
Received of John Alsop 16d.
Received of William Blank 16d.
Received of William Frebrige [no sum given]
Received of John Freman [no sum given]
Received of Richard Brysbe [deleted]
Received of Christian (*Krystion*) Luscher for this 3 year 3s.
Received of John Leke 12d.
Received of William Robarttys, boardmaker, for the 2 past years 12d.
Received of northern [*sic*] John's wife in part payment of a fine of 6s. 8d. paid 8d.
Received of Geoffrey Morton for this year 6d.
[f. 60v.] Memorandum received of the brothers towards the charge of the barge going with the sheriffs to Westminster for a covered boat the 18th year of the king [Henry VII 1502–1503]
Robert Ettell 12d.
John Alsop 8d.
John Blanche 4d.
William Blank 4d.
Received of John Bowman for a fine following the judgement of Master Chamberlain 6s. 8d.
Received of John Wekys for a fine for tarrying after his hour at the Greyfriars 8d.
Received of John Alsop for the same reason 8d.
Received of Thomas Michell for the same reason 8d.
Received of David Greffythe for the bequest of his master on his death bed 8d.
Received of Thomas Michell for sending to the Chamber 4d.
Received in quarterage of the yeomanry [114] 35s.
Received of John Ross for his woman 20d.

60. [f. 61] The account of Robert Ettell, umper, John Alsop and William Blank, umpers and wardens of the craft of wiresellers who gave their account in the Wiresellers' Hall in the twenty-third year of King Henry VII [August 1507- August 1508]
First received at the last account 2s.
Received of Robert Cadman 12d.
Received of John Alsop 2s.
Received of John Ross 12d.
Received of William Kell for 2 years 12d.
Received of John Thorp in part payment of his quarterage 4d.

114. See introduction, p. xix.

Received of Nicholas Horner for quarterage for which he was in arrears 4s.
Received of William Frebrige for his 2 servants for John Heggy and John Smyth 3s. 4d.
Received of John Bowman as a fine for his servant Richard Belyngle 20d.
Received of Thomas Vynsent for his quarterage 6d.
[f. 61v.] Received of John Strode for his servant William Brathwate to be admitted as a workman 20d.
Received of Robert Ettell for his servant, Thomas Adurtton to be admitted as a workman 20d.
Received 15 June 21 Henry VII [1506] for 4 worn torches 13s.
Received of William Blawull, by full agreement of the company in the hall 40s.
Received for Elizabeth Ettell to become a sister 20d.
Received of John Wright to be admitted as a whole brother 40d.
Received of Richard Beaumont to become a brother 40d.
Received of William Ettys to be admitted a brother 40d.
Received of John Awston to be admitted a whole brother 40d.
Received for quarterage for 3 years from the whole company £3 4s. 2d.
Item received of Thomas Poterell for his fine to be admitted as a journeyman with occupation 20d.

61. The payments of Robert Ettell, John Alsop and William Blank as appears by bills:
To William Rogerrys, waxchandler 7s. 4d.
Item paid to the waxchandler for burying [Robert] Chenwyth's wife and for John Freman 11s. 9d.
Item paid to the waxchandler for our light at the Whitefriars as appears by his bill 12s. 8d.
[f. 62] Item paid to the Whitefriars for 3 trentals of masses over the last 3 years 7s. 6d.
Item paid to the sexton of the Whitefriars for trimming our light of the brotherhood 4d.
Item paid to the friars for a trental of masses for Robert Chenwyth's wife 2s. 6d.
Item paid to the parson of St Alban in Wood Street[115] in the first payment for the whole of the past year 3s. 6d.
Item paid to the same parson our offerings on two occasions 3s. 6d.
Item paid to the wardens of the Taylors for our Hall the past 3 years £3
Item paid for our Hall to the king's *fyllnyrr*[116] for 3 years 6s.
Item paid for darning and washing our table cloths at various times 4d.
Item to a clerk to write our bills at various times 4d.

115. Richard Skipwith, parson 1505–1519.
116. Probably filacer: officer of the superior courts at Westminster in charge of filing and processing original writs.

Item paid for a burden of rushes and for coals at various times 5d.
Item paid to the beadle, Robert [Skydmore], for 3 years 18s. 8d.
Item paid to the writer for the *birt* with the bills 12d.
Delivered at the account in the Wiresellers' Hall to the new umpers and wardens 18s. 6d.

62. [f. 63] The account of Robert Ettell, John Wright and Richard Beaumont, the umpers and wardens of the craft, presented in the Wiresellers' Hall
16 September 2 Henry VIII [1510].
In primis received of the old wardens 10s. 8d.
Item received for a kilderkin of ale given by John Strode 9s.
Item received of John Powell to be admitted a workman 20d.
Item received of Edward Flede to be admitted as a workman 20d.
Item received of John Jarret for old quarterage 2d.
Item received of Robert Cowll for old quarterage 6d.
Item received of Richard Hasyllhurst to make him a freeman 6s. 8d.
Item received of John Strode the younger to make him a freeman 6s. 8d.
Item received of Richard Beaumont to make his wife a sister 20d.
Item received of John Wright's wife to make her a sister 20d.
Item received of John Trowlre in part payment of his fine to make him a freeman 20d.
Item received of John Pawllmerr to make him a whole brother 3s. 4d.
Item received of Agnes Cadman to make her a sister 20d.
Item received of John Torner for old debts 20d.
Item received of all brothers in the company 25s. 9d.

63. [f. 64] The payments
Memo[randum]: Paid by the umpers and wardens first for bringing the mayor to Westminster and back 8s.
Paid to Michael Waklyn for washing and darning our cloths 3d.
Paid for papers and writing of the quarter roll 2½d.
Paid to Sir John Rogers curate of St Alban church [Wood Street] 3s. 6d.
Paid to the wardens of the Taylors for our hall for a whole year 20s.
Paid for the light at the burying of John Bowman 8d.
Paid for a breakfast in our hall when the mayor went to Westminster 2s.
Paid to the waxchandler for a whole year 14s. 9d.
Paid to the beadle for a whole year's wages 6s. 8 d.
Paid for setting in [to the tables] of the brothers and sisters 2d.
Paid for the writing of the account 6d.
So remaining, all charges paid and delivered into the box to the new wardens 20s. 10d.

64. [f. 64v.] The account of Robert Cadman, John Wright and John Strode the elder, umper and wardens of the craft of Wiresellers, presented to the

company on 23 September 3 Henry VIII [1511] who delivered into the box 34s.
Remaining to the craft and company in quarterage 30s.
[There are no further entries]

[There follows the petition and ordinances of the Pinners and Wiresellers as granted by the City on 2 March 1497][117]

65. [f. 65v.] [Latin] Memorandum that, on 2 March, 12 Henry VII [1497], the wardens of the mystery of the Pinners and of the craft of Wiresellers of the City of London and other good men of the said mysteries, came to the King's court in the hall of the Guildhall of the city of London, to the court of John Tate, the mayor, and aldermen and presented the mayor and aldermen with a bill or supplication in the following words:

[English] To the right honourable the Mayor and his worshipful brethren the Aldermen of the City of London, the poor fellowships of the crafts of Pinners and Wiremongers enfranchised in this City humbly [appeal] to your honourable lordship and wisdoms:
that whereas the said fellowships heretofore often and diverse times have vied, vexed and sued each other for certain points concerning both the said fellowships to the great and insupportable charge of the same, both now being of very small numbers and in such great poverty and decay that they can no longer maintain their fellowships, nor to bear scot and lot, nor other charges as they have done heretofore, they now show here they are so poor that they cannot any longer continue to maintain or keep up their said fellowships [for fear of] their utter destruction and to the hurt and hindrance of divers other fellowships in the city.
[f. 66] Considering the foregoing, [may] it please your good lordship and masters to grant to your said supplicants that both the said fellowships may be made one, to be named the craft of Wiresellers, and utterly to dismiss and anull the names of Pinners and Wiremongers. And that it may be lawful for the brethren of the Wiresellers annually to elect, on the day following the feast of the Assumption of Our Lady [15 August], an Umpire and two Wardens, to see that all the good rules and ordinances made and enacted by the fellowship of the Wiresellers may be duly kept and executed, as in every craft within the city.
And also that you will grant to your said supplicants that all the articles hereafter ensuing, which were granted by your court to the crafts of Wiremongers and Pinners, as is a matter of record, may remain firm and stable, to be enacted and granted to the said craft of Wiresellers. This in [due] reverence to God and charity and your said supplicants shall daily pray to God for your lordship and masterships.

117. See *LBL*, pp. 319–321; London Metropolitan Archives, Corporation of London Letter Book L folios 329–331 where the wording is slightly different, but the substance of the articles is the same.

66. [f. 66v.] [The ordinances of the Wiresellers]

No man to work on Saturdays or vigils after 3 o'clock

No person of the craft shall work on Saturday nor on the vigil of a double feast after 3 o'clock in the afternoon on pain of paying two pounds of wax, or 8d for the pound; one half of the fine to the Chamber and the other half to the use of the craft.

Every man to answer all summons

Also that every freeman of the craft shall obey all the summons which the umper and wardens shall think necessary for the weal of the fellowship and the profit of the city. And [if] any person absent himself from such summons without lawful cause he shall forfeit two pounds of wax or else 16d. of which one half to the Chapel of the Guildhall of London and the other half to the use of the craft.

All to be obedient to the umper and wardens and no man to rebuke another

[f. 67] Also that every freeman of the said craft shall, from henceforth, obey the umper and wardens and no brother thereof shall rebuke or revile any other brother by any dishonest language in the presence of the umper and wardens or among the fellowship of the craft upon pain of paying 3s. 4 d. for each offence: one half of which to go to the Chamber and the other half to the fellowship.

No man shall be hired out of his house, shop or standing place in market or fair.

No man of the craft shall hire another of the same craft out of his dwelling house, or shop or standing place at any market or fair upon pain of forfeiting or paying at every default 5 marks to be applied to the use of the Chamber and craft as aforesaid.

To desire no man's servant out of his master's service

Also that no man of the craft shall procure or entice into his service any servant in covenant with this craft out of the service of his master, within the time of his said service; upon pain of paying 13s. 4 d. for each such default: the money to be divided as before.

No freeman of the craft to work with any person who is not enfranchised in the same craft

[f. 67v.] No freeman of the craft to work with anyone within the franchise of the city, nor take any work that belongs to the craft, but only with and of such persons as have been made free of the craft, without licence of the umper and wardens for the time being, so that he may have competent work and wages within the said fellowship, on pain of a fine of 20 shillings to be divided as before.

That no man set any person to work openly in his shop

No freeman to work, or set to work, any person openly in his shop in the *wyndyng* of buckles, cutting of stones for moulds, scoring of the same, graving the molds, casting of metal or colouring of the same, whereby anyone not a member of the fellowship, might learn the said occupations and skills; nor is the freeman to show or teach these skills to anyone outside the fellowship except to his wife, children, apprentices and covenanted servants who have been apprentices in the craft, without the agreement and licence of the umper and wardens, on pain of a fine of 6s. 8d. to be divided as before.

No foreigners to keep house or shop until admitted as a freeman

Also no foreign may hold house or shop in the city or its suburbs, nor buy nor sell anything connected [f. 68] with the craft until such time as he has been examined by the umper and wardens of the time as to whether he is able to work and occupy the craft and to become a freeman of the city: upon pain of forfeit for each such default 6s. 8d. to be divided as before.

No foreigner to be set to work until presented before the umper and wardens

Also no foreign may work in the craft within the franchise of the city until he is presented by a freeman of the craft to the umper and wardens and there be examined of his doings: thereupon they will ordain reasonable wages, weekly or annual, such that the master may maintain his estate and the said servant live decently (*honestly*). And that no such foreign may take or set to work any apprentice or other servant on the work of the craft until he himself be admitted to the freedom of the city: upon pain of a fine of five marks. And no freeman of the craft may set such a foreign to work until he has been duly presented: upon pain of a fine of another five marks, to be applied to the uses already described.

Every foreigner to pay 3s. 4d. at his presentation and to swear to observe the good rules of the craft

[f. 68v.] Also that every such foreign, at his presentation, shall pay to the umper and wardens 3s. 4d., to be applied as aforesaid: and anyone sworn before the umpers and wardens is to obey and fulfil all the good rules and ordinances of the craft, here approved by the court, and shall pay all such fines and penalties as are laid down and contained in these ordinances as often as he shall break or disobey the same rules and ordinances, or any of them.

No man to entice or receive another man's servant

Also that none of the fellowship may procure or cause to be procured, secretly or openly, or receive, any servant, apprentice or *allowe* of any other person in the fellowship by which the master shall be the worse served, either by night or by day: upon pain of a fine for such default of 40s., to be divided as above described. And if any servant be eloigned or taken away then it shall be lawful for his master, without any offence, to take him back again.

Anyone who misbehaves and will not be corrected to be dismissed

Also if any of the craft be of evil disposition and guiding and accustomed to do ill and will not be reformed by the good people of the craft, and if he be convicted of falsehood to the value of 12d., he is to be utterly forsaken and put out of the fellowship until such time as he may have the grace to amend himself: and if any person of the fellowship [f. 69] take on any such misadvised person into his service without the licence of the umper and wardens, he shall forfeit each time 6s. 8d., the money to be applied as described.

No man to hold open shop on Sunday

Also no person of the craft is to open shop on a Sunday, but if any stranger wishes to buy his merchandise on that day he shall cause him to come to his house and there show him his wares, in order to accommodate travellers. And if he goes against this [rule] he will pay 3s. 4 d. each time, to be divided as before.

No man to entice or call away merchants or chapmen from others

Also that no man of the craft shall call away or entice any merchant or chapman from the house, shop, stall or booth of any other member of the fellowship within this city or in any other place, fair or market, upon pain of a fine of 6s. 8d., to be divided as aforesaid.

No man to employ a woman unless she is his wife or daughter

Also that no member of the craft set any woman to work other than his wife or daughter, upon pain of a fine of 6s. 8d. to be divided as before.

Every foreign woman to pay 3s. 4d.

[f. 69v.] Also that no woman, being a foreign, may work at anything pertaining to the craft until such time as she pay 3s. 4d. to be divided as before.

No-one to work at noisy work except as specified hours

Also no man to work in the said craft [involving] knocking, filing or any other disruptive (*noyfull*) work whereby his neighbours and other king's subjects may be annoyed or disturbed (*diseased*) during the [period] from the feast of Michael the Archangel [29 September] to that of the Annunciation of Our Lady [25 March] but only from the hours of 5 o'clock in the morning until 8 o' clock in the night, upon pain of a fine of 3s. 4d. to be divided as before.

The umper and wardens may make due search of any man's wares

Also it shall be lawful for the umper and wardens of the said craft, and successors, to make due search in all necessary and convenient places in the city and the suburbs of all kinds of wire goods: English pins, clasps, eyelets (*auletts*), pack needles, buckles, chains, fish hooks, stock cards, hand cards and everything pertaining to the craft of wiresellers, in the hands of whoever has them and wherever found. And every parcel of the said wares the umpers and wardens find to be insufficient or unworkmanlike shall be forfeited and presented by the umpers and wardens to the chamberlain of the city.

No man to hawk his wares

[f. 70] Also it shall not be lawful for any person of the craft, nor anyone on their behalf, to go hawking, or to proffer their wares for sale at any inn or other place within the franchise of the city, upon pain of a fine of 6s. 8 d. for each offence, to be divided as before.

A light and mass to be kept at the White Friars, and the umper and wardens to be chosen on the day following the feast of the Assumption of Our Lady [15 August]

Also the said umper and wardens and the fellowship may have, and keep, their light in the Whitefriars in Fleet Street, in the suburbs of London, to burn in honour of God, Our Lady St Mary, St James and St Clement: and every year, on the feast of the Assumption of Our Lady [15 August] to attend the Mass there and on the morrow to elect and choose the umper and wardens for the next year. And at no time hereafter will it be lawful for the said umpers and wardens, their successors nor any of the rest of the craft to keep the light or attend the mass in any place but in Whitefriars, without the agreement of the mayor and aldermen of the city. And he that disobeys will forfeit £10 sterling each time he does so.

[f. 70v.] [Latin] And when the mayor and aldermen had read and more fully understood the bill or supplication, and as it seemed to the same mayor and aldermen that the articles in the said bill or supplication were good and honourable and consonant with reason, by the assent and will of all, they ordained and decreed that the aforesaid articles should be entered here as of record in the manner and form by which they are to be strictly observed in future times.

APPENDIX 1

Pinners' and Wiresellers' Wills

67. (GL MS 9051/1 f. 5) RICHARD ALEYN
Pinner 1372 (listed only)

68. (GLMS 9051/1 f.15) STEPHEN CHILD
Citizen and pinner 1384 (listed only)

69. (GLMS 9171/1 f.342) JOHN atte HILLE 9 June 1395
[Latin]
1. I John atte Hille, citizen and pinner of London, being of good memory write my testament in this manner. First I commend my soul to Almighty God, my creator, to the Blessed Mary his mother and to all the saints.
2. My body to be buried in the cemetery of the church of St. Bride's in Fleet Street, in the suburbs of the city where I am a parishioner, outside the north part of the church next to the tomb of Alice, my wife.
I leave 6s. 8d. to the high altar of St. Bride's for oblations forgotten and not paid.
I also wish that all my debts shall be faithfully paid from my goods.
5. I bequeath 12d. to whoever is chaplain to celebrate [mass] daily in the church and for a sermon next to my body.
6. I bequeath 6d. to whoever is parish clerk of the said church.
7. I leave to John Ayleston, my kinsman, two of my best pieces of silver except one piece and twelve silver spoons.
8. Also to John Ayleston my kinsman I leave all the remaining term which I have in the tenement with its appurtenances in which I live in Fleet Street aforesaid with all the remaining terms of all my apprentices, to have and to hold the remaining term of the said tenement with appurtenances to the said John Ayleston my kinsman and his assigns.
9. I give 6s. 8d. to John Bilton.
10. And I leave 8 marks to my executor for the funding of one honest chaplain to celebrate mass for my soul for one whole year after my death in the aforementioned church and for the soul of Alice my wife and for the souls of those I hold dear.
11. The residue of all my goods not previously bequeathed I give and leave to the said John Ayleston that all my said debts be acquitted and to dispose

for my soul and the burial of my body, as it shall please God and for the salvation of my soul.
12. I make and declare John Ayleston my executor.

70. [GLMS 9051/1 f.148] JOHN DAWNTRE 31 October 1405
[Latin]
1. I John Dawntre, citizen and pinner of London, being of sound mind and in good memory do write, ordain and make my present last will and testament in this manner. First I leave and commend my soul to Almighty God, the Blessed Virgin Mary, his mother and to all the Saints.
My body to be buried in the cemetery of the church of St Martin Pomeroy in Ironmonger Lane, London.
3. I desire that, first and foremost after my burial, all and singular the debts for which I am responsible be paid.
4. I leave to the high altar of the said church for my tithes and oblations overlooked, withheld or kept back 20d.
I leave towards the stipend of a certain chaplain of this church, to pray for my soul on the day of my obit 2d.
I leave to Walter, the parish clerk of the church 8d.
7. The true residue of all my goods and chattels, wherever they may be, after the payment of my debts and my legacies, I give and leave to Joan, my wife, for her to do with and dispose of by her free will, to provide prayers for my soul and also for the distribution of my goods and chattels among my sons, as she pleases.
8. And I make and constitute my faithful executors, viz. my said wife, Joan the principal executrix, John Stodely, tailor, and Laurence Gorlefen, citizen and pinner of London, to whom I entrust the faithful execution of this present testament.
Witnesses: Thomas Cave, joiner, John Howell, John Becleton, pinner and John Cadyn, purser and William Goddishall, needler.
Probate granted 9 November 1405

71. (GLMS 9171/2 f.79) JOHN STOKES 6 October 1406
[Latin]
1. I John Stokes, citizen and pinner of London, in healthy mind and good memory make, ordain and constitute this my present testament in this fashion. First I leave my soul to Almighty God and to the Blessed Virgin Mary his mother and all the saints.
2. My body to be buried in the great cemetery of St Paul's cathedral London where my executors choose and I desire that the expenses thereof be at the wish and disposition of Agnes, my wife.
3. And I leave to the high altar of St Peter in Westcheap London for tithes and oblations forgotten and unpaid 2s.
I leave towards the fabric of the nave of the said church 3s. 4d.
5. The true residue of all and singular my goods and chattels, moveable and immoveable, wherever they may be, not bequeathed, my debts having been paid, I give and bestow on Agnes, my wife, to dispose of for me and for the good of my soul, as seems best to her, and for the sustenance, training and

upbringing of John, my son, and also asking her to do all she can for the support of Alice, my daughter, now remaining in Coventry.
6. And I declare the said Agnes, my wife to be my principal executrix and also Laurence Gorlefen, pinner and Walter Prendretas, fruiterer and citizens of London to be executors of this testament. For their labours in this part I wish them to have 6s. 8d., that is to each of them 40d.
Probate granted 9 December 1406

72. (GLMS 9171/2 f.103) WILLIAM UPTON 27 August 1407
[Latin]
Died intestate, apparently without family, of the parish of St. Lawrence, Jewry, at a time of plague. Administration granted to the vicar of his parish church, Robert Winbwell.[118]

73. (GLMS 9051/1 f.271) JOHN STANES 10 December 1411
[Latin]
1. Memorandum that John Stanes, being in good and sound mind, spoke and declared his testament orally in the following way. First he bequeathed his soul to Almighty God, to St Mary the Virgin and all the Saints.
His body to be buried in the cemetery of his parish church, St Mary Somerset in London.
He left 4d. to Master John, chaplain in the said church of St Mary.
4. He also bequeathed all his goods, moveable and immoveable, wherever they might be, to Alice his wife for the payment of his debts, for the salvation of his soul and the souls of all the faithful departed.
5. To ensure that his will is faithfully observed, he made and constituted his wife, Alice, his executrix.
6. Witnessed by John Wayte, Thomas Clerk and John Dalby.
Probate granted 15 October 1412

74. (GLMS 917112 f.325v) JOHN CHESTER 18 November 1415
[Latin]
1. I John Chester, citizen and pinner of London, sound in mind and memory, write, make and ordain this my present testament in this way. First I give and recommend my soul to Almighty God, my Creator, and to the Blessed Mary his mother and to all the Saints.
2. My body to be buried in the church of St Martin Pomeroy in Ironmonger Lane, London.
3. I leave to the high altar of the said church, for my tithes and oblations forgotten 15d. I give to whoever is chaplain of the same church to pray for my soul and for the souls of those I hold dear and for all the faithful departed 4d.
4. I leave to Alice, my wife, £20 and all my jewels.

118. Robert Wombwell, vicar of St Lawrence Jewry 1394–1419, see A.B. Emden, *A Biographical Register of the University of Oxford to A.D. 1500* (Oxford, 1958), pp. 2080–2081.

5. And to John Chester, my son, I leave 10 marks, six silver spoons and my best furred gown.
6. To my craft of pinners in London I leave 6s. 8d.
7. I bequeath to Laurence Proute, citizen and pinner of London, a quarter die to draw wire pertaining to his craft
8. I leave the residue of all my goods and chattels, after the settlement and payment of all my debts and my legacies fully paid, to Alice my wife, for her to sell and I desire that the money arising shall be disposed of in pious uses and charitable works for my soul and for those souls aforementioned, as she thinks best.
9. And I make executors of this my testament the aforementioned Alice as principal executrix and William Grymmsby, girdler, and Laurence Gorlefen, citizen and pinner of London: each to have for his labours 10s.
Probate granted 24 November 1415

75. (GLMS 9171/2 f.370v) LAURENCE GORLEFEN 17 August 1417 [Latin]
1. I Laurence Gorlefen, citizen and pinner of London, sound in mind and memory do write, make and ordain this my present testament in this form. First I give and recommend my soul to Almighty God, to the Blessed Virgin Mary his mother and to all the Saints.
2. My body to be buried in the cemetery of the Friars Minor in London and I leave the same friars 6s. 8d. to celebrate [mass] for my soul.
3. I also leave to Master John, as parish chaplain of the church of St Matthew in Friday Street London, to celebrate [mass] for my soul 3s. 4d.
4. All the residue of my goods after the payment of my debts and my legacies fulfilled I give to my executors, written below, to dispose for my soul as they see best.
5. And I make Elena, my wife, my principal executrix and Richard Maidstone, citizen, my executor.
6. Witnessed by Laurence Proute, pinner, Richard Moore, tailor and William Nicholl, tallow chandler.

76. (GLMS 9171/3 f.153B) THOMAS UNDERHILL 11 September 1422 [Latin]
1. I Thomas Underhill, citizen and pinner of London, of sound mind and good memory, praise to the Almighty, do make my testament in this form. First I bequeath and commend my soul to Almighty God my Creator and to the Blessed Virgin Mary his mother and to all the Saints.
2. My body to be buried in the body of the nave of the church of St Mary Magdalene in Milk Street, London, and for my funeral and special prayers for my soul l0s. to the said church.
3. I leave 3s. 4d. to St Mary Magdalene in Milk Street for my tithes and oblations forgotten or withheld and for the rector of the said church to pray for my soul.
4. I leave 8d. to whoever is chaplain in the same church to pray for my soul and 8d. to the other clerks of the same church to pray for my soul.

5. I leave 3s. 4d. towards the maintenance of the fabric of the church of St Augustine in the parish of Kingston on Thames.
6. I leave to Stephen, canon of Tybere[119] in county Essex, my relative, six silver spoons to pray for my soul.
7. And I leave to John Underhill, my brother, of Kingston 6s. 8d., a gown with a hood from my own clothes, following the discretion of my executors, to pray for my soul.
8. I leave each of my sons and daughters in the city of London and elsewhere within the realm of England, 12d.
9. I leave to Dionisia, daughter of John Underhill, who resides with me, one pair of linen sheets, one blanket, one coverlet of a bed, my second best brass pot and 6s. 8d. to pray for my soul.
10. I leave to Roger Underhill, my brother, 6s. 8d. and a robe with a hood from my own clothes following the good discretion of my executors to pray for my soul
11. To the community of the Fraternity of the Assumption of the Blessed Virgin Mary de Rouncivall, near Charing Cross,[120] of which fraternity I am a member, 6s.8d. for gowns for each of the brothers so that they recommend my soul to God in their prayers.
12. I leave to the fraternity of my craft of Pinners 20s. for gowns for each of them who come to my funeral and to do for my soul as they do for the other brothers and to recommend my soul to God in their prayers and, at the discretion of my executors, I do release and pardon all those who are indebted to me and by the fortune of the world have lost their goods and have nothing from which to pay the debt.
13. And I give to John Stanes of London, pinner, my kinsman who is staying with me, that he will be my executor with Margaret my wife, one bed with coverlet, one pair of blankets, one pair of sheets and six silver spoons: one pair of mazers decorated with silver, half a dozen of my pewter vessels, one brass pot, one brass bowl, a hundred of wire and half of all the tools of my trade for his good labour and diligence in this matter.
14. My debts and funeral expenses paid, all my [remaining] goods to Margaret, my wife, to dispose of as she thinks best to please God and for the good of my soul.
Probate granted 10 March 1425

77. (GLMS 9171/3 f.315v) WILLIAM REDGATE, pinner, 6 November 1432
[Latin]
Administration granted to John Colzon, girdler and William Studell, pinner.

119. Possibly the hospital of East Tilbury, see *The Victoria Histories of the Counties of England: Essex*, vol. ii (1907), p. 191.
120. See Barron and Davies, *Religious Houses,* pp. 232–233.

78. (GLMS 9171/3 f.376) ALICE BYSET 10 April 1434
[Latin]
Administration of the goods of Alice Byset granted to Thomas Byset, pinner

79. (GLMS 9171/3 f.376) STEPHEN DRAX, pinner, 13 April 1434
[Latin]
Administration granted to widow whose name is lost in the binding [Alice?].

80. (GLMS 9171/4 f.63) JOHN TAYLOR 19 December 1436
[Latin]
1. I John Taylor, citizen and pinner of London, being of sound mind and good memory, set down, make and ordain my present testament in this manner. First I commend my soul to Almighty God my Creator and to the Blessed Virgin Mary his mother and to all the Saints.
2. My body to be buried in the cemetery of St Mary [*recte* Martin] Pomeroy in Ironmonger Lane, London.
3. I desire that all my debts be paid at once after my burial.
4. I leave 12d. to the High Altar of the church of St Martin for tithes and oblations forgotten and unpaid.
5. I leave to Robert, the son of my sister Agnes 20d.
6. I leave to William, the son of my sister Margaret, 12d.
7. The true residue of all my goods wherever they may be after the payment of all my debts and funeral expenses I give and bequeath wholly to Emote, my wife, for her to spend and distribute for the benefit of my soul.
8. I declare and ordain as my executors the said Emote and John Milford, citizen of London, and I give to the said John Milford 6s. 8d. for his labour.
Probate granted 19 June 1441

81. (Husting Roll 170/64) JOHN HILL (senior) 7 October 1437
[Latin]
1. I John Hill senior, citizen and pinner of London, being in good memory, do ordain and make my present final testament in this manner, viz. I give my lands, tenements with shops, solars and cellars, with all their appurtenances, situated in the parish of St Bride Fleet Street, in the suburb of London, between Bride Lane in the parish aforesaid to the west, the tenement held of late by Adam Carlill on the east, and up to the house of the abbot and convent of Winchcombe on the south, and the King's highway of Fleet Street to the north, which was lately held by the gift and enfeoffment of Roger Sapurton, esquire, warden of the King's prison of the Fleet, John Ullesthorp, citizen of London, master William Prys, priest, Robert Croke and John Hill, junior, citizens of this city, as is made clear in a certain deed of mine.
2. Firstly I leave to Thomas Franks, rector[121] of the said parish of St Bride Fleet Street and to Richard Skerning and Thomas Tryll, his churchwardens,

121. Thomas Faux, rector of St Bride, Fleet Street by 1437; died 1459.

all those lands, tenements with shops, solars and cellars, except 3 shops with their solars and appurtenances situated in Bride Lane and closely adjacent to the gate of the hospital or house of the abbot and convent of Winchcombe to the north, which are reserved for John Hill, junior, citizen and esquire, his heirs and assigns; to have and to hold all the said lands and tenements with shops, solars and cellars, except those aforesaid, to Thomas Franks, rector and his successors and Richard Skerning and Thomas Tryll, churchwardens and their successors of the said church, for ever, under the conditions below.

3. That every year, forever, after my decease, on the eve and day of St Mary Magdalene, they hold a special anniversary, specifically celebrating the service of the dead with three sung masses, including one for the Holy Trinity and another for the Blessed Virgin Mary, for my soul and for the soul of Joan, late my wife, and for the souls of all the faithful departed, particularly for the souls of those most dear to me. To each one of the chaplains who takes part in these services 4d., and the said anniversary to be accompanied with torches and the ringing of bells. And if the rector and his chaplains take part in the service and mass then the rector to receive 12d. and the chaplains 6d. And the clerks of the parish for their labour and bell-ringing to have 18d., viz. 12d. for the bell-ringing and 6d. for the service and mass

4. Also I will that 5s. 6d. from the profits of the said lands, tenements and shops be distributed to the poor, weak and greatly needy by the rector and churchwardens and their successors

5. And also to the honour of God and that the chaplain who lately celebrated in the chantry in the church of St Bride for the souls of John Wygan and Joan his wife[122] be well and sufficiently supported, I will that Thomas Franks, rector and the churchwardens and their successors pay annually to the chaplain 20s. from the profits of the said lands, tenements and shops, forever, at the four terms of the years according to the customs of the city of London. And the chaplain should celebrate and hold divine service as is written below: viz. within the octave of the feast of Christmas there should be three full masses including the *Gloria in Excelsis Deo*, a special collect of St Gregory, and the service of the dead. The said chaplain should also perform the antiphon of the blessed Mary in the said church in his vestments unless he is not able because of troubles or infirmities. And finally the said chaplain should hold a full service within the octave of nine other feasts, namely Epiphany, Purification, Annunciation, Easter, Ascension Day, Pentecost, Trinity Sunday, Assumption of the Virgin Mary and the Nativity of the Virgin Mary following the customs of those feasts just as was celebrated and done in the aforesaid octave of Christmas, for my soul and the soul of Joan my late wife and all the faithful departed.

6. And should the said lands fail to produce 20s. *p.a.*, wholly or in part, then the chaplain may, at his discretion, distrain on the annual rents of the lands, tenements, shops, solars and cellars aforesaid to meet the deficit and to cover any costs and expenses he incurs. Or if it is not possible for this or

122. For this chantry, see C. Kitching ed., *London and Middlesex Chantry Certificate* (London Record Society, 1980), no. 107.

some other chaplain to perform the services as described then the rector and churchwardens to retain the 20s. and distribute one half to the poor and greatly needy of the parish for my soul, the soul of Joan my late wife and all the faithful dead and I leave the other half to the fabric of the church of St Bride.
7. To this my present testament I affix my seal, John Michell then being Mayor of London and William Hales and William Chapman then being sheriffs of London
Witnesses to the will: William Venour, Robert Byston, Augustine Hawkins, Henry Longope, Henry Ragle and others
Probate granted 16 July 1442

82. (GLMS 9171/4 f.23) JOHN HILL 7 July 1439
[Latin]
1. I John Hill, citizen and pinner of London, being of sound mind and good memory, do make my testament as follows. I leave and commend my soul to Almighty God, my Creator and Saviour, to the Blessed Virgin Mary, his mother, and to all the Saints.
2. My body to be buried in the tomb next to my late wife, Joan, in the chapel of St Anne, under the parish church of St Bride's in Fleet Street, in the suburbs of London.
3. I leave to the high altar for tithes and oblations overlooked 40d.
4. I leave 20d. for the maintenance of a light in the chapel of St Mary the Virgin in the same place
5. I leave 20d. to the maintenance of the light of St Cross in the same place
6. I give to the fabric of the [cathedral] church of St Paul's 40d.
7. I leave to the church of St Bride's one iron chest
8. I leave to John Hill my kinsman my best large mazer.
9. And I leave Alice, lately the wife of John Hill, my brother, my second best mazer.
10. I leave to John Wells my best gown.
11. I leave to John Bulcell my second best gown.
12. The true residue of all my goods not bequeathed above I leave to the disposal of John Wells, pinner, and John Hunt, tailor and citizen of London. I desire and require that they may act according to my will and dispose of a pair of bed-hangings and my vessels of copper and brass only, as well as they can, for the profit and benefit of John Hill, my aforesaid kinsman.
13. I make the said John Wells and John Hunt executors of my present will; to apply the money raised from my goods for the soul of Joan, my late wife, and for those souls I hold dear. And I leave each of them 20s. for their labours.
Probate granted 21 July 1439

83. [GLMS 9171/4 f.195] JOHN WELLS 18 June 1446
[Latin]
1. I John Wells, citizen and pinner of London, in good memory, praised be the Almighty, do make, ordain and constitute my present testament and last

wishes as follows. First I bequeath my soul to Almighty God, my Creator, and to the Blessed Virgin Mary, his mother, and to all the Saints.
2. My body to be buried in the burial ground of St Bride the Virgin in Fleet Street London, near Alice, my former wife, and my son.
3. I desire that all my debts, whether [enforceable] by law or [good] faith, shall be paid completely.
4. The true residue of all my goods and chattels, after my said debts are paid, I leave and give to Margaret, my wife, freely to dispose of as she thinks best for my soul in charitable works best pleasing to God and for the health of my soul.
5. And 1 declare and ordain the said Margaret principal executrix of this my will and Thomas Hatfeld, citizen of London, supervisor.
Probate granted 13 August 1446

84. [GLMS 9171/4 f.243v) JOHN EDRYCH 1 February 1443
[Latin]
1. I John Edrych, citizen and pinner of London, sound of mind and in good memory do write make and ordain this my last will and testament in the following manner. First I bequeath to Almighty God my Creator and Saviour and to the Blessed Mary his mother and to all the saints.
2. My body to be buried in the church of St Botolph without Aldersgate in London at the discretion of my executors written below.
3. And for the works on the body of the said church and my burial there I leave 6s. 8d.
4. I leave to the high altar of the church in exoneration of tithes and oblations overlooked 12d.
5. And I desire that all my debts be settled immediately after my burial and my funeral expenses to be paid by my executors.
6. The true residue of all my goods, after my debts legacies and burial have been settled, I leave totally to Emma, my wife, for her and Thomas Plot to dispose of for my soul as seems best to them.
7. I make and ordain the said Emma, my wife, and the said Thomas Plot my principal executors and John Joye, citizen of London. And I leave to John Joye 20s. for his labours.
Probate granted 29 September 1448

85. (GLMS 9171/5 f.286v) ROBERT VICARY 25 October 1459
[Latin]
1. I Robert Vicary, citizen and pinner of London, of sound mind and healthy memory, praise be to the Almighty, do write make and ordain my present testament in this way. First I leave and recommend my soul to Almighty God, my Creator and Saviour, to the Blessed Virgin Mary, his mother, and to all the Saints.
2. My body to be buried in the church of St Sepulchre, wherever God, in his supreme grace, wishes to put me; and I desire that my body be honestly buried with the minimum of pomp.
3. I wish that my debts, all and singular, wherever and to whomever they may be owed, be faithfully and wholly met,

4. I leave to the high altar of St Matthew Friday Street, London, for tithes and oblations forgotten and unpaid and in exoneration of my soul 12d.
5. And I leave two torches, at the discretion of my executors and to the same high altar, for the veneration of Corpus Christi, and for as long as they last.
6. I also leave to each of the orders of the Austin Friars, the Carmelites and the Friars Minor of London 6s. 8d., that they may celebrate a trental mass and will sing by note that my soul be specially recommended to God.
And I leave to the prisoners of Ludgate and Newgate, London, 3s. 4d. in bread.
I leave to Isabel my servant 6s. 8d.
9. I leave to John Vicary, my son, 40 pounds sterling made up of 20 pounds in good legal money of England, and goods and materials of my trade to the value of 20 pounds, to be given and delivered to him without question, at the discretion of my wife.
10. The true residue of my goods and chattels, after the payment of my debts, my aforementioned funeral expenses and of this testament, I give and leave wholly to Alice, my wife, that she may dispose of it for the good of my soul and for the souls of those I hold dear, in pious uses and charitable works.
11. I make, ordain and constitute the aforementioned Alice my principal executrix and William Michell, citizen and pinner of London, and John Jenkyn, citizen and mercer of London, as co-executors. And I leave each of them 20s. for their labours in this matter.
12. I also leave my Antiphoner,[123] for the praise and honour of God in the chancel of the church of St Matthew aforesaid, that is to say in the north part of the chancel, so that the parish may pray especially for me, for as long as it lasts.
Probate granted 8 November 1459

86. (GLMS 9171/5 f.296v-97) WILLIAM STODELL 20 May 1460
[Latin]
1. I William Stodell, citizen and pinner of London, sound of mind and in good memory, make, write and ordain my testament and will in this manner. First, I leave and commend my soul to Almighty God, my Creator and Saviour, to the Blessed Virgin Mary and to all the Saints.
2. My body to be buried in the great cemetery of the church of St Paul's London, in the place where my sons lie buried.
3. I leave to the high altar of the parish church of St Michael in Wood Street, where I am a parishioner, 12d. for tithes and oblations forgotten and withheld.
4. I leave to Robert Page, citizen and embroiderer of London, and to Anabel, his wife, 10 marks.
5. And I leave to Letitia Page, daughter of the said Robert, 6s. 8d. and to John Page son of the said Robert 6s. 8d.

123. The Antiphonal contained most of the music required in church services.

6. I leave 18 marks for one suitable, good and honest chaplain to be found to celebrate [mass] for the next two years at the altar of the chapel of St Mary in the aforesaid church of St Michael, for my soul and for the souls of Roger Stodell, my father, and Anabel, my mother, and all my friends and benefactors and all the faithful departed, immediately after my death; the chaplain to be paid at the four terms of the year by the hand and discretion of my executors.
7. I also desire that my executors well and faithfully following their good and sensible discretion, give, dispose and distribute to twelve paupers and women in great need, by their hands, in the parish of St Michael Wood Street, aforesaid, twelve quarters of coal at the feasts of All Saints and the Annunciation, for the term of 10 years following my death.
8. I also desire my feoffees who with me and Margaret my wife, in great confidence have been enfeoffed with a certain tenement with its appurtenances situated in the town of Ware in the county of Hertford, which was lately held and occupied by Annabel Vynde, my mother, now dead, immediately after my death to make, or cause to be made, to the said Margaret my wife a good, true and legal document of release from all the interest which they have in the said tenement and appurtenances; all of this to be done and performed without delay by anyone and according to my will and pleasure as written in this present testament.
9. I desire that all my debts which I owe to anyone be settled and satisfied, and, at the discretion of my executors, my funeral expenses and legacies fulfilled.
10. The residue of all my goods after my debts paid, funeral expenses and legacies fulfilled I give and leave entirely to Margaret, my wife, for her to dispose of freely and at her discretion for ever.
11. I hereby make and ordain my executors, Margaret, my wife, Robert Page aforesaid and William Michell, citizen and pinner of London, and Nicholas Bynde, citizen and currier of London, to be supervisor. And I give William Michell 20s. for his labour in this matter and to Nicholas Bynde 20s.
Probate granted 27 June 1460

87. (GLMS 9171/5 f.392–92v) GEOFFREY PRANY 30 August 1466 [Latin]
1. I Geoffrey Prany, citizen and pinner of London, of sound mind and good memory, compose make and ordain my present testament and last will in this way. First I give and recommend my soul to Almighty God my Creator and to St Mary the Virgin and to all the Saints.
And my body to be buried in the cemetery of the cathedral church of St Paul's London.
3. I leave 2s. to the high altar of the church of St Magnus on the Bridge, of which I am a parishioner, in payment of tithes and oblations omitted.
4. I also leave 12d. to the high altar of the church of St Vedast in Westcheap, London.
5. I leave 12d. to the fraternity of the Holy Cross in the church of St Peter in Westcheap.

6. I leave to Robert my son 40s., a *dublet de defence*, one *axe isalet*, one pair of gauntlets, a pair of good linen sheets, 1 pair of blankets, a coverlet and one good mattress, to be delivered to him when he comes of age.
7. I leave the custody of these goods and money to Joan my wife for so long as she does not marry. And should it happen that my wife Joan die or remarry before Robert is of age, then I wish my brother, Thomas Prany, the supervisor of this testament of mine, to have the custody of the said money and goods belonging to Robert when he comes of age. And should he die, then I wish Henry Felde, fletcher, and Henry Somer, pinner, citizens of London and supervisors of my present testament, to arrange for the custody of the money and goods for the profit of the said Robert and answering to him when he comes of age
8. And should the said Robert die before coming of age, then I leave the said money and goods for disposal, for the good of my soul, the souls of my wife, and son, Robert, and all the faithful departed
9. I leave to the said Thomas Prany, my brother, my dark red gown lined with marten fur
10. I leave to Richard Andrew, lately my master, my murrey gown lined with black sheepskin and 1d. each week for the rest of his life
11. I leave to Thomas Boges, pinner, 5s.
12. The rest of all my goods, chattels and debts, my debts and funeral expenses being paid and this present testament fulfilled, I give entirely to Joan, my wife, whom I do make and constitute the executrix of this testament, and as supervisors of this testament I appoint the aforesaid Thomas Prany, Henry Felde and Henry Somer, to each of whom I give 3s. 4d. for their labour.
Probate granted 6 October 1466.

88. (GLMS 9171/5 f.388–88v) GEOFFREY WADE 12 September 1466 [English]
1. I Geoffrey Wade, citizen and pinner of London, of the parish of St Katherine's Christchurch, being in whole mind, ordain and make this my present testament in manner and form following. First I bequeath my soul to Almighty God and to the most Glorious Virgin his mother, St Mary, and to all the Saints of Heaven.
2. My body to be buried where God will dispose best for me, at the discretion of my executors.
3. I give to the high altar of the parish church of St Katherine's Christchurch 3s. 4d.
4. Also, if it can be met, I will that a priest of honest conversation pray for me devoutly for a whole year, or to have a trental to the sum of 10 marks for his salary.
5. I give and bequeath my grayle[124] to the said parish church of St Katherine, for evermore.

124. A grail or gradual: a book containing all the music sung by the choir during the mass.

6. I give and bequeath to my son, Thomas Wade, and equally to everyone of my daughters, 5 marks of my silver plate or in other of my goods.
7. I give my son William Wade 20s.
8. I give my wife's best gown and best girdle to Alison Wade, my daughter.
9. The second best girdle and gown to my daughter Joan Godewyn.
10. And the third gown and girdle to my daughter Katherine Stanmpe
11. I also give and bequeath to William Herbert 10 marks in money and his terms [of apprenticeship?] to be disposed of by my executors underwritten.
12. I give to John, my apprentice, 20s.
13. I give and bequeath to Alison Wyndham 20s. in money.
14. And I straightly require and charge each of the said children, as they shall answer at the High Day of Judgement, that none of them sue, trouble or vex any of my executors, in so much that I have given and bequeathed unto each and every of my said children their portions of their goods before this time except to my son, Thomas Wade, who never received his part of my goods, to whom I give and grant, by the present writings, all my goods and debts not bequeathed in this my present testament, my own debts paid first and my legacies carried out.
16. I ordain and make my chief executor the said Thomas Wade, my son, he only to dispose, administer and fulfil my testament and last will in all things.
17. And I ordain and make his co-executors Richard Froste, fruiterer, and Thomas Godewyn, girdler and citizen of London, to support my said son in his disposition of all my goods, and if there are any challenges to this my testament and last will.
18. I give and bequeath to the said Richard [Froste] and Thomas Godewyn 20s. to each of them for their labour in this matter.
Probate granted 18 September1466

89. (GLMS 9171/6 f.24v-25) RICHARD HUGHIS 29 April 1468
[Latin]
1. I Richard Hughis, citizen and pinner of London, being of sound mind and good memory, Almighty God be praised, write, make and ordain my present testament in this manner. First I give and commend my soul to Almighty God; my Creator and Saviour, to the Most Blessed Mary, his mother, and to all the Saints.
2. My body to be buried next to the tomb of John St John, in the north cemetery of the parish church of St Bride the Virgin in Fleet Street, in the suburb of London.
3. I desire, first and foremost, that all and singular my debts, which I owe to anyone, be settled in full.
4. I leave to the said church for my tithes and oblations overlooked 5s.
5. I desire that 30 masses be celebrated for my soul as soon as possible after my death.
6. I remit, pardon and release John Davell from the two final years of his term of apprenticeship, on condition that the said John remains the faithful and obedient apprentice of Margaret, my wife, and that the said John faithfully serves the said Margaret or her assigns during the remainder of his

apprenticeship after my decease, except for the final two years, and that he pays the said Margaret for all the care and expenses that I Richard paid and incurred when John left my service and had to be re-apprenticed.
7. I leave to my apprentice John Foster 26s. 8d., to be delivered to him at the end of his apprenticeship, on condition that he continues to serve Margaret, my wife, or her assigns, for the whole of the rest of his apprenticeship after my death.
8. I leave to my apprentice John Leche 6s. 8d., to be delivered to him at the end of his apprenticeship, on condition that he serves the said Margaret faithfully to the end of his apprenticeship.
9. The true residue of all my goods, after my legacies and debts are paid, and my funeral covered, I leave wholly to Margaret, my wife, to do with freely as she wishes, to use and dispose of them, for the good of my soul, as seems best to please God,.
10. I make and ordain Margaret, my wife, principal executrix of my present testament and William Almer, citizen and haberdasher of London, and Thomas Vaux, of London, sergeant, co-executors.
11. And I leave to each of them, William and Thomas, for their labours 6s. 8d.
Probate granted 4 July 1468

90. (GLMS 9171/6 f.130) JOHN CADMAN 2 April 1472
[Latin]
1. I John Cadman, of sane mind, sick in body, commend my soul to Almighty God, to the Blessed Mary and all the Saints.
2. My body to be buried in the church of St Sepulchre.
3. I leave to the high altar in my parish church for tithes forgotten 16d.
4. I leave to William, my son, 20s.
5. And to Robert, my son, 20s. and my best gown.
6. The residue of all my goods I bequeath to Alice, my wife, for her to dispose of for the good of my soul, as she thinks best.
7. I make my wife my sole executrix of my will and Edmund Legge to be supervisor: he to have 10s. for his labours.
Sealed in the presence of Master William Clerk, chaplain of the parish, William Crendon, Edward Sulby and others.
Probate granted 22 July 1472

91. (GLMS 9171/6 f.122–22v) JOHN RONELL 7 October 1472
[Latin]
1. I John Ronell, citizen and pinner of London, and of sound mind and of good memory, Almighty God be praised, do write, make and ordain this testament in the following manner. First I give and commend my soul to Almighty God, my creator and saviour, to the Blessed Virgin Mary, his mother and to all the Saints.
2. My body to be buried in the cemetery of St Paul's cathedral in London, if possible, where the body of Joan, my late wife, lies buried.
3. I desire that my debts should be truly settled.

4. I leave to the high altar of the parish church of St Mary Magdalene in Milk Street London, where I am a parishioner, 12d. for my tithes and oblations forgotten.
5. The true residue of all and singular my goods and chattels not already bequeathed, the cost of my burial met and the whole of this testament fulfilled, I leave wholly to Isabel my wife and also to my children, Thomas and Alice, to be divided between them, in the manner and custom of the city of London.
6. I make, ordain and name the said Isabel the sole executrix of this my present testament and John Vicary, citizen and pinner, to be supervisor.
I leave the same John Vicary 6s. 8d. for his labour in this matter.
8. And finally to all and singular I give notice by this my present testament that, on account of the sound choice and great confidence which I had in Edmund Legge, citizen and pinner of London, a certain Edward Lunsey, lately of Shinglewell in the county of Kent, esquire, John Charlton, of the same place, yeoman, and Henry Dannell, of the same place, husbandman, who owe me £8, and Geoffrey Craft of Shinglewell, aforesaid, husbandman, and John Crower, husbandman of the same place, who also owe me £10, have been bound and held by their two bonds in the said sums to me and the said Edmund for my use only and not for the use of that Edmund, on account of which I will, require and desire through my present testament that the said Edmund Legge, at no time in the future, invoke any legal action through my executrix or her executors against my said debtors or to seize any of them for non-payment of the sums aforesaid or any part thereof, nor make any acquittal or discharge of the same or any part thereof without the consent of my executrix or her executors. And finally the same Edmund should not meddle with the receipt of the aforesaid sum or any part thereof.
Probate granted 12 November 1472

92. (GLMS 9171/6 f.220) MARGARET STODELL 23 December 1477 [Latin]
1. I Margaret Stodell, widow of London, being in clear mind and good memory make my testament in this manner. First I give and commend my soul to Almighty God my Creator and Saviour, to St Mary the Virgin his mother and to all the Saints.
2. My body to be buried in the cemetery of St Paul's cathedral, London, next to where the body of William Stodell, citizen and pinner of London, my late husband, lies.
3. I leave to the altar of the church of St Michael in Wood Street London, where I am a parishioner, 6s. 8d. for tithes and oblations forgotten.
4. And I leave 3s. 4d. for the high altar of St Peter's in Westchepe.
5. 1 leave to the fraternity of St Cross in the same church 3s 4d.
6. I give to the fabric of the said St Paul's cathedral 6s.8d.
7. The true residue of all my goods, chattels and debts, wherever they may be, after my debts are settled, my funeral paid for and the legacies of this testament fulfilled, I give and bequeath wholly to Robert Page, citizen and broiderer of London, and to Anabel his wife, to share with the children of

their daughters, and for distribution in works of charity and mercy for the good of my soul as they wish

8. I ordain Robert Page and Anabel his wife my just and faithful executors.

Probate granted 12 February 1478

93. (GLMS 9171/6 f.257–57v) JOHN VICARY 1 March 1478
[Latin]

1. I John Vicary, citizen and pinner of London of sound mind and in good health and memory, thanks be to the Almighty, do compose, make and ordain my present testament in the following manner. First I give and recommend my soul to God Almighty and to the Blessed Virgin Mary, his mother, and to all the Saints.

2. My body to be buried in the cemetery of the church of St Matthew the Apostle in Friday Street, London, next to the body of Robert Vicary my father.

3. I leave to the high altar of the said church, for exoneration of tithes and oblations forgotten and unpaid 3s. 4d.

4. The true residue of all and singular of my goods and chattels, not bequeathed and after the payment of all my debts, the legacies of this testament fulfilled and my funeral expenses fully paid, I give and leave in full to Isabel, my wife, and I make and constitute her my sole executrix of this testament of mine, and Peter Walpole and Thomas Wymark co-executors: and I leave to each of the said executors 6s. 8d. for their labours in this matter. And James Terumbere of Bradford in the county of Wiltshire, clothman, to be supervisor of this testament.

Witnesses: Nicholas Edwards, chaplain, John Worlych, Thomas Colard.

Probate granted 26 April 1479

94. (GLMS 9171/6 f.332) ROBERT RUMBOLD 7 April 1482
[Latin]

1. I Robert Rumbold, citizen and pinner of London, of sound mind and healthy memory, thanks be to the Almighty, compose, make and ordain my present testament in the manner following: first, I leave and commend my soul to Almighty God my creator, to the Blessed Virgin, Mary his mother, and all the Saints.

2. My body to be buried in the nave of the parish church of St Peter in Westcheap, London.

3. I leave for the fabric of the nave of the church towards my burial 6s. 8d.

4. I leave to the rector of the said church in compensation for tithes forgotten and withheld 3s. 4d.

5. I leave to the fraternity of the Holy Cross in the same church that the brothers and sisters of the same may pray for my soul 3s. 4d.

6. The true residue of all my goods and chattels not bequeathed above, my debts resolved, my funeral paid for and my testament performed, I wish to be distributed and disposed of by Christina, my wife, and Thomas Rumbold, citizen and mercer of London, for the good of my soul and the souls of my parents, of my friends and all the faithful departed, in the celebration of masses and in other pious uses and charitable works, at the

discretion of Christina, my wife, and Thomas Rumbold whom I name and constitute my executors.
7. I leave to Thomas Rumbold 13s. 4d. for his labour in this matter.
8. I desire that my executors shall sell all my lands and tenements, called Soward and Fronde, which I hold by a copy of the roll in the lord's court of Southminster in the county of Essex; my son, Thomas Rumbold, to have 5 marks of the money from their sale, to be given him at the age of 21.
9. And if the said Thomas should die before that age, then I leave the said 5 marks to Edmund Rumbold, my son, if he is still alive then, otherwise I wish the said 5 marks to be divided equally between his children. And if both Thomas and Edmund and all his children die, the said 5 marks should be distributed in pious uses and charitable works.
10. I leave to Isabel Smyth, daughter of John Smyth, 20s. towards her marriage, from the aforementioned sale of lands and tenements.
11. And I desire that all the rest of the money from the sale should be distributed and disposed of by my executors as they see best for my soul and to please God.
Probate granted 20 March 1482

95. (GLMS 9171/8 f.224) WILLIAM PARKER 3 August 1500
[English]
1. I William Parker, citizen and wireseller of London, in whole and good mind, laud and honour be to Almighty God, make and ordain this my present testament, containing my last will, in manner and form following. First I bequeath and recommend my soul to Almighty God, my Saviour, and second to Our Blessed Lady St Mary, his most glorious mother, and to all the holy company of Heaven.
2. And my body to be buried in the church of the Whitefriars in London, before the image of St Alban, on the south side of the said church.
- 3. I bequeath to the high altar of St Alban [Wood Street], for offerings which were behindhand, withheld or forgotten 3s. 4d.
I leave to Alice, my sister, John Benet's wife, 20s.
5. I also wish that my executors, written below, dispose in bread at the time of my burial 6s.8d. and a barrel of good ale.
I give to all those who have been and who are my apprentices 6s. 8d. each.
7. I give my executors full power to sell all such plate as I have for the best price they can and with the money thereof to fulfil my will in every particular.
8. I bequeath to Stephen Palow a riding gown of tawney lined with deep tawney.
9. I give to Isobel Quille, widow, in ready money 3s. 4d.
10. I give to John Alsop, citizen and wireseller of London, after my decease, a close of land and wood, called Coldwater, within the lordship of Harringay, containing 3 acres and a rod, in the county of Middlesex.
11. I bequeath to William Benet, after the decease of Emma, my wife, one cottage with a curtilage and a garden, late of William Frend, and two acres of land lying in Highgate in the said lordship of Harringay. And if it turns out that the said William Benet is not virtuous and good, and of good

guidance and rule, then I wish my executors to sell it, as well as they can; half of the money to be disposed in charitable works and mercy, as they think most fit for the good of my soul, and the other half to go towards the mending of the highways between Highgate and St John's corner where is most need.
12. I bequeath to Emma, my wife, for her life, a cottage with a curtilage in Highgate, within the lordship of Harringay. And after her decease, it is to pass to my sister Alice, the wife of John Benet, and after his decease, to go to William Benet, her son, if he be of good rule and good guidance. [If not,] to my said executors to sell and to dispose of the money ensuing for my soul and the soul of Emma, my wife, and for all true Christian souls.
13. I leave to the said Emma, my wife, a cottage with a curtilage called Sitwells in Highgate Green Lane; John Barret and Margery, his wife, and their assigns to have it for ever.
14. The residue of all my goods to my wife, for her to dispose of as she thinks best and needful, for the good of both our souls and all Christian souls.
15. I ordain and make John Alsop, wireseller, and Henry Hill, haberdasher, executors of this my last will and testament and I leave each of them 20s
Witnessed by: the parson of St Alban [Wood Street],[125] William Founteyn, Richard Surcock, leatherseller.
Probate granted 12 November 1500

96. (GLMS 9171/9 f.89v) JOHN WEKYS 26 May 1518
[English]
1. I John Wekys, citizen and pinner of London, being sick in my body and whole in my mind, thanks be to God, make and ordain this my present testament in form following. First I bequeath my soul to Almighty God my maker and to Our Lady St Mary and all the Holy Company of Heaven.
My body to be buried in St [Bride's] church before the north door and nigh to the holy water stoop.
3. I bequeath to the brotherhood of Our Lady in the said church of St Bride £10, which [was given by] Thomas Wyson, groom of the chamber to our lord King Henry VIII, now being with his Grace, if the said brotherhood will sue for it; as will be shown in a good obligation, which shall be delivered by my overseer for me, so that the said brotherhood will pray for me.
4. I bequeath to John Hyams, my servant, his freedom, he to pay the fee to the Chamber [of the Guildhall].
5. I also bequeath to Thomas Petre, my servant, his freedom, he to pay the fee to the Chamber [of the Guildhall].
6. I give Joan, my maid, 5s.
7. I bequeath to my lad Raphael 5s.
8. All the residue of all my goods, moveable and immoveable, my funeral paid and my body buried, I freely give to Jane, my wife. I make and ordain her my sole executrix for the performance of my will

125. Walter Smith, parson of St Alban's Wood Street, 1498–1502, see Emden, *Biographical Register*, p. 1720

9. I make and ordain John Johnson my overseer, for the performance of my will and I bequeath him for his labour my best furred gown with a hood. Witnessed by: Sir Humfrey Towne, my spiritual father, Edward Tate and Master Sympkotte
Probate granted 5 June 1518.

97. (GL MS 9171/9 f. 181) ROBERT DRURY 5 May 1521
[English]
1. I Robert Drury, citizen and wireseller of London, sick in body nevertheless whole in mind and in perfect remembrance thanks be to God, make and ordain this my last will and testament as follows. First I bequeath and recommend my soul to Almighty God, my maker and redeemer, to his glorious mother Our Lady St Mary the Virgin and to all saints.
2. And my body to be buried in the church yard of St Benet Gracechurch as near as possible to the grave of John Wheler.
3. I bequeath to the high altar of St Benet for forgotten or withheld tithes, 12d.
4. I leave to Elizabeth Drury, my daughter, 53s 4d. when she reaches lawful age or marries. If she dies before this, then the 53s. 4d. to remain to my wife Agnes to dispose of in deeds of charity for my soul as she thinks best.
5. I wish my executors, immediately after my death, to have five masses of the five wounds sung and said at the Scala Coeli within the Convent Church of the Crossed Friars.
6. I leave to Nicholas Capper my best bow.
7. I leave the residue of all my goods, chattels and debts, after my debts have been paid and my testament fulfilled, to Agnes my wife whom I appoint as my sole executor.
8. I leave to Thomas Notte, grocer and to John Shepard, waxchandler, 3s. 4d. each, desiring them to help my executor.
9. Witnessed by: Thomas Notte and John Shepard and Henry Standish, notary.
Probate granted 15 June 1521

98. (GL MS 9171/10 f.174) WILLIAM FREBRIGE 21 January 1529
[English]
1. I William Frebrige, citizen and wireseller of London, being in good health and whole mind, laud and praise unto Almighty God, make and ordain and dispose this my present testament and last will in manner and form following. I give and recommend my soul to Almighty God my maker and redeemer, and to the most glorious Virgin his Mother, Our Lady St Mary, and the whole company of heaven.
2. And my body to be buried in an honest manner within the parish church of St Stephen Coleman Street, London, where the body of Margery, my wife, lies buried, or as near to the same place as may be conveniently done.
3. I give and bequeath to the high altar of the church of St Stephen Coleman Street for my tithes and oblations forgotten or withheld in discharge of my soul 20d.

4. I give and bequeath to my daughter Ann Howman, the wife of Richard Howman, shearman, a house at a rental of 6s. 8d. or else 6s. 8d. yearly to be paid by my son John Frebrige, or his assigns, for the term of my daughter Ann Howman's life.
5. I leave the residue of my goods, movable and immovable after my debts are paid and the costs of my burial done and my testament fulfilled, to John Frebrige, my son, and to Richard Howman my son in law, whom I make and ordain my executors.
Witnessed by: Richard Ketyll, vicar of the aforesaid parish church, James Hill, Thomas Serle and diverse others.
Probate granted 23 October 1531

99. (GL MS 9171/14 f.85–85v) WILLIAM EDGEBOROW 1 September 1558
[English]
1. I William Edgeborow of the parish of St Sepulchre without Newgate, pinner, diseased and sick in body, but of good and profitable memory and remembrance, laud and praise to Almighty God, do make and ordain this my present testament and last will as follows. I give and commend my soul into the hands of Almighty God, the Father, Son and Holy Ghost, in whom and by whom and in whose merited and precious death, in the name of the Father, Son and Holy Ghost, I trust and believe assuredly to be saved and to have full and clear remission and forgiveness of my sins
2. And I commit my body to the earth to be buried in Christian burial at the discretion of my executors.
3. I give and bequeath to my son Thomas Edgeborow, all my lease, interest and term of years of my dwelling house where I now dwell, for the rest of the term of years now to come, to have and enjoy the same to him, and to the heirs of his body lawfully begotten. And if the said Thomas, my son, should die without issue, then I will that the remainder of the same lease shall go to my daughter Joyse Huwe and to her children lawfully begotten. And if the same Joyse shall die without issue, then the remainder of the lease shall go to my cousin Margaret Grove, now the wife of Nicholas Grove, and the issue of her body, if the term of years contained in the said lease shall so long continue.
4. I give and bequeath to Thomas Taylor, my son in law, my gown furred with fox fur, a platter and a dish of pewter, and a candlestick of latten, and also the third part of my moulds of my occupation of pinner that I cast with.
5. I give and bequeath to the said Joyse, my daughter, a great kettle and an iron pot.
6. I will that my executors shall pay every year after my decease to Margaret Grove, my cousin, 3s 4d. out of [the income from] my dwelling house during the continuation of the said lease, provided always that if my said son Thomas, after my decease, shall not be minded to dwell in and occupy my said house himself, but be minded to sell or otherwise do away with the said lease given to him, then I will that the said Joyse shall immediately enter into my said house and enjoy the same lease according to the gift made to her.

7. The residue of all my goods and other things not already bequeathed, I will shall remain to my son Thomas Edgeborow, whom I make my sole executor.
8. And to see my will truly accomplished, I ordain and make my trusty friend John Starkeford, salter of London, overseer to see that right may be done to my said children as my trust is in him. I give to him for his pains, two platters of pewter.
Sealed on the day above written in the presence of Morgan Lydde, scrivener.
Probate granted 1 January 1559

APPENDIX 2

Wardens of the Pinners and Wiresellers

Those wardens for whom a will has survived are marked *.

Wardens' names recorded in the city's Letter Books

1356 (*LBG*, p. 64)	John atte Hill*	Stephen Child	John Stafford	Ralph Weltone
1371/2 (*LBG*, p.290)	William Callere	William Coventre	Benedict Mills	Richard Fletbrigge
1377/8 (*LBH*, p.77)	John Goman	Adam York		
1378/9 (*LBH*, p.97)	William Coventre	John Dawntre*		
1379 (*LBH*, p.132)	John Stafford	John Dawntre		
1380 (*LBH*, pp. 151–2)	John Higham	William Castell		
1381 (*LBH*, p.170)	Hugh Bromhille	William Coventre		
1383 (*LBH*, p.222)	John Bilton	William Bokeler		
1386 (*LBH*, p.292)	John Hereford	William Callere	Benedict Mills	
1388 (*LBH*, p.337)	John Bilton	John Stanes*	John Rede	Laurence Gorlefen*
1389 (*LBH*, p. 346)	John Chapman	William Bokeler		
1390 (*LBH*, p. 356)	John Rede	Laurence Gorlefen	John Chapman	
1391 (*LBH*, p. 369)	John Hill	John Chester*	John Byset	
1392 (*LBH*, p. 389)	John Dawntre	Robert Laundene		
1394/5 (*LBH*, p. 417)	John Rede	John Byset	John Chester	
1416 (*LBI*, p. 172)	Richard Maidstone	Laurence Gorlefen	William Brembill	
1418 (*LBI*, p. 207)	Thomas Underhill*	Laurence Proute	John Dowe	
1421 (*LBI*, p. 287)	John Hill	John Brewer	William Brembill	
1423 (*LBK*, p.30)	Thomas Underhill	Richard Maidstone	Thomas Manger	
1441 (*LBK*, p. 257)	Geoffrey Wade*	William Stodell*	John Couper	
1452 (*LBK*, p. 344)	William Michell	Thomas Byset*	William Clerk	

The names of Umpers and Wardens of the Pinners as they appear in the Pinners' and Wiresellers' Book

	Umpers	Wardens	
1462–64	Geoffrey Wade	John Vicary*	Edmund Legge
1464–66	William Machon	Henry Somer	Robert Rumbold*
1466–68	John Couper	Edmund Legge	Thomas Tarte
1468–70	William Michell	John Vicary	John Bartlet
1470–72	Henry Somer	Robert Rumbold	John Plays
1472–75	William Machon	Edmund Legge[126]	John Bartlet
1475–77	John Vicary	ThomasTarte[127]	Robert Hill
1477–81	Robert Rumbold	John Bartlet	William Parker*
1481–83	John Plays[128]	William Parker	Robert Howton
1483–87	William Machon	John Bartlet	John Wekes*
1487–91	William Parker	Robert Ettell	Richard Tweke[129]
1491–92	John Bartlet	John Wekes	John Stoneham
1492–95	William Machon	John Wekes	Robert Ettell
1495–97	William Parker	Robert Ettell	Robert Chenwyth
1497[130]	William Parker	Ralph Underwood	William Blank

The names of Umpers and Wardens of the Wiresellers as they appear in the Pinners' and Wiresellers' Book

1497–99[131]	Robert Ettell	Robert Cadman	Ralph Underwood
1501	John Blanche	John Alsop	William Frebrige*
1504	John Wekys	Thomas Michell*	Thomas Rawlyn
1507	Robert Ettell	John Alsop	William Blank
1509–10	Robert Ettell	John Wright*	Richard Beaumont
1510–11	Robert Cadman	John Wright	John Strode

126. Robert Rumbold replaced Edmund Legge who died
127. Replaced by John Plays
128. John Plays died in office
129. Replaced by John Stoneham
130. These last wardens of the independent Pinners' Company rendered an account for the period from 20 April to 15 August 1497 (**42**)
131. Their account begins 24 August 1497 (**46**)

INDEX

References in Roman numerals are to pages in the introduction: other references are to paragraph numbers in the text.

LONDON RECORD SOCIETY

The London Record Society was founded in December 1964 to publish transcripts, abstracts and lists of the primary sources for the history of London, and generally to stimulate interest in archives relating to London. Membership is open to any individual or institution; the annual subscription is £18 (US $22) for individuals and £23 (US $35) for institutions. Prospective members should apply to the Hon. Secretary, Dr Helen Bradley, London Record Society, PO Box 691, Exeter, EX1 9PH (email londonrecordsoc@btinternet.com)

The following volumes have already been published:

1. *London Possessory Assizes: a calendar*, edited by Helena M. Chew (1965)
2. *London Inhabitants within the Walls, 1695*, with an introduction by D.V.Glass (1966)
3. *London Consistory Court Wills, 1492–1547*, edited by Ida Darlington (1967)
4. *Scriveners' Company Common Paper, 1357–1628, with a continuation to 1678*, edited by Francis W. Steer (1968)
5. *London Radicalism, 1830–1843: a selection from the papers of Francis Place*, edited by D. J. Rowe (1970)
6. *The London Eyre of 1244*, edited by Helena M. Chew and Martin Weinbaum (1970)
7. *The Cartulary of Holy Trinity Aldgate*, edited by Gerald A. J. Hodgett (1971)
8. *The Port and Trade of early Elizabethan London: Documents*, edited by Brian Dietz (1972)
9. *The Spanish Company*, edited by Pauline Croft (1973)
10. *London Assize of Nuisance, 1301–1431: a calendar*, edited by Helena M. Chew and William Kellaway (1973)
11. *Two Calvinistic Methodist Chapels, 1748–1811: the London Tabernacle and Spa Fields Chapel*, edited by Edwin Welch (1975)
12. *The London Eyre of 1276*, edited by Martin Weinbaum (1976)
13. *The Church in London, 1375–1392*, edited by A. K. McHardy (1977)
14. *Committees for the Repeal of the Test and Corporation Acts: Minutes, 1786–90 and 1827–8*, edited by Thomas W. Davis (1978)

15. *Joshua Johnson's Letterbook, 1771–4: letters from a merchant in London to his partners in Maryland*, edited by Jacob M. Price (1979)
16. *London and Middlesex Chantry Certificate, 1548*, edited by C. J. Kitching (1980)
17. *London Politics, 1713–1717: Minutes of a Whig Club, 1714–17*, edited by H.Horwitz; *London Pollbooks, 1713*, edited by W.A. Speck and W.A. Gray (1981)
18. *Parish Fraternity Register: Fraternity of the Holy Trinity and SS.Fabian and Sebastian in the parish of St. Botolph without Aldersgate*, edited by Patricia Basing (1982)
19. *Trinity House of Deptford: Transactions, 1609–35*, edited by G.G.Harris (1983)
20. *Chamber Accounts of the sixteenth century*, edited by Betty R. Masters (1984)
21. *The Letters of John Paige, London Merchant, 1648–58*, edited by George F. Steckley (1984)
22. *A Survey of Documentary Sources for Property Holding in London before the Great Fire*, by Derek Keene and Vanessa Harding (1985)
23. *The Commissions for Building Fifty New Churches*, edited by M.H.Port (1986)
24. *Richard Hutton's Complaints Book*, edited by Timothy V. Hitchcock (1987)
25. *Westminster Abbey Charters, 1066-c. 1214*, edited by Emma Mason (1988)
26. *London Viewers and their Certificates, 1508–1558*, edited by Janet S. Loengard (1989)
27. *The Overseas Trade of London: Exchequer Customs Accounts, 1480–1*, edited by H.S.Cobb (1990)
28. *Justice in Eighteenth-century Hackney: the Justicing Notebook of Henry Norris and the Hackney Petty Sessions Book*, edited by Ruth Paley (1991)
29. *Two Tudor Subsidy Assessment Rolls for the City of London: 1541 and 1582*, edited by R.G.Lang (1993)
30. *London Debating Societies, 1776–1799*, compiled and introduced by Donna T. Andrew (1994)
31. *London Bridge: selected accounts and rentals, 1381–1538*, edited by Vanessa Harding and Laura Wright (1995)
32. *London Consistory Court Depositions, 1586–1611: list and indexes*, by Loreen L.Giese (1997)
33. *Chelsea settlement and bastardy examinations, 1733–66*, edited by Tim Hitchcock and John Black (1999)
34. *The church records of St Andrew Hubbard Eastcheap, c. 1450-c. 1570*, edited by Clive Burgess (1999)
35. *Calendar of Exchequer Equity pleadings, 1685–6 and 1784–5*, edited by Henry Horwitz and Jessica Cooke (2000)
36. *The Letters of William Freeman, London Merchant, 1678–1685*, edited by David Hancock (2002)
37. *Unpublished London diaries. A checklist of unpublished diaries by Londoners and visitors, with a select bibliography of published diaries*, compiled by Heather Creaton (2003)
38. *The English Fur Trade in the later Middle Ages*, by Elspeth M.Veale (2003; reprinted from 1966 edition)

39. *The Bede Roll of the Fraternity of St Nicholas*, edited by N.W. and V.A. James (2 vols., 2004)
40. *The estate and household accounts of William Worsley, Dean of St Paul's Cathedral, 1479–1497*, edited by Hannes Kleineke and Stephanie R. Hovland (2004)
41. *A woman in wartime London: the diary of Kathleen Tipper 1941–1945*, edited by Patricia and Robert Malcolmson (2006)
42. *Prisoners' Letters to the Bank of England 1783–1827*, edited by Deirdre Palk (2007)
43. *The Apprenticeship of a Mountaineer: Edward Whymper's London Diary 1855–1859* edited by Ian Smith (2008)
44. *The Pinners' and Wiresellers' Book 1462–1511* edited by Barbara Megson (2009)

Many volumes are still in print; see http://www.londonrecordsociety.org.uk.